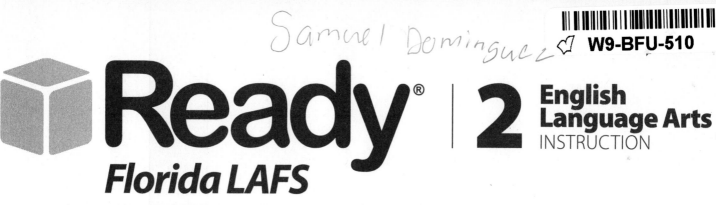

Ready® | 2 English Language Arts
Florida LAFS
INSTRUCTION

Samuel Dominguez

W9-BFU-510

SIMPLE MACHINES

ELECTRICITY IS ALL A...

TWISTERS

INSECTS

SHADOW

THE FOOD W...

OCEAN LIFE

Deep Sea W...

A TRIP TO THE RAIN FOR...

AMPHIBIONS

Poems About Weather

All About Rocks

EXPLORING THE EAR...

Vice President of Product Development: Adam Berkin
Editorial Director: Katherine Rossetti
Executive Editor: William Kelleher
Project Manager: Audra Bailey
Editors: Melissa Brown, Anne Cullen, John Ham, Rob Hill, Susan James
Cover Design: Matt Pollock
Cover Illustrator: O'Lamar Gibson
Design/Production: William Gillis, Mark Nodland, Lisa Rawlinson, Jennifer Sorenson, Jeremy Spiegel

NOT FOR RESALE

ISBN 978-1-4957-0557-1

Acknowledgments

Barbara Hesson, "A Prickly Adventure," Copyright © 2008 by Highlights for Children, Inc., Columbus, OH.

Adapted from "Native American Inventions." Published in *Scholastic News*, November 7, 2004. Copyright © 2004 by Scholastic Inc. Used by permission.

Adapted from "Squanto and the Pilgrims." Published in *Scholastic News*, December 18, 2007. Copyright © 2007 by Scholastic Inc. Used by permission.

"Seeds Get Around" by Kate Hofmann. © 2012 National Wildlife Federation. Reprinted from the October 2012, *Ranger Rick*® magazine, with the permission of the copyright owner, the National Wildlife Federation®.

Levine, Shar and Leslie Johnstone, excerpt from *First Science Experiments: Wonderful Weather*. Copyright © 2003 by Shar Levine and Leslie Johnstone. Reprinted with permission by Sterling Publishing Co., Inc.

"Operation: Rescue Possum" by Charnan Simon, *Click*, February 2011. All Cricket Media material is copyrighted by Carus Publishing Company, d/b/a Cricket Media, and/or various authors and illustrators. Any commercial use or distribution of material without permission is strictly prohibited.

Adapted from "Abe Lincoln's Cabin" by Dara Sharif. Published in *Scholastic News*, February 18, 2008. Copyright © 2008 by Scholastic Inc. Used by permission.

"Kids on the High Seas" by Dave and Jaja Martin, *Click*, March 2009. All Cricket Media material is copyrighted by Carus Publishing Company, d/b/a Cricket Media, and/or various authors and illustrators. Any commercial use or distribution of material without permission is strictly prohibited.

Adapted from "Apple Picking Time" by Dara Sharif. Published in *Weekly Reader*, Edition 2, September 1, 2010. Copyright © 2010 by Scholastic Inc. Used by permission.

"Picnic Guests" by Cynthia Reeg, *Ladybug*, August 2012. All Cricket Media material is copyrighted by Carus Publishing Company, d/b/a Cricket Media, and/or various authors and illustrators. Any commercial use or distribution of material without permission is strictly prohibited.

Elizabeth Tidy, "My Lizard," Copyright © 2008 by Highlights for Children, Inc., Columbus, OH.

Eileen Spinelli, "I Love the World," Copyright © 2011 by Highlights for Children, Inc., Columbus, OH.

"The Shade Seller: A Korean Folktale" by Marilyn Helmer, *Spider*, March 2012. All Cricket Media material is copyrighted by Carus Publishing Company, d/b/a Cricket Media, and/or various authors and illustrators. Any commercial use or distribution of material without permission is strictly prohibited.

Reena I. Perl, "The Squirrel and the Crow," Copyright © 2005 by Highlights for Children, Inc., Columbus, OH.

Rhonda Leverett, "Kate Skates," Copyright © 2011 by Highlights for Children, Inc., Columbus, OH.

From *Recycle That!* by Fay Robinson. All rights reserved. Reprinted by permission of Children's Press, an imprint of Scholastic Library Publishing Inc.

Xu Li, "Gu Dong Is Coming!" Copyright © 2010 by Highlights for Children, Inc., Columbus, OH.

The Ugly Truckling by Dave Gordon. Copyright © 2004 by David Gordon. Used by permission of HarperCollins Publishers.

Common Core State Standards © 2010. National Governors Association Center for Best Practices and Council of Chief State School Officers. All rights reserved.

Language Arts Florida Standards (LAFS) © 2014. Florida Department of Education.

Table of Contents

*Standards in **boldface** are the focus standards that address major lesson content.*

*Standards in **boldface** are the focus standards that address major lesson content.*

Table of Contents continued

*Standards in **boldface** are the focus standards that address major lesson content.*

Language Handbook

Conventions of Standard English

Knowledge of Language

Vocabulary Acquisition and Use

Unit 1

Key Ideas and Details in Informational Text

Have you ever looked at the moon and wondered about it? Maybe you have asked questions like these: How far away is the moon? When did astronauts first land on the moon? What did they find there?

In this unit, you will read and ask questions about different topics, such as where and how different animals live. You will learn to see how important events and ideas in history and science go together. You'll also learn how steps in directions can help you make and do things.

✓ Self Check

Before starting this unit, check off the skills you know below. As you complete each lesson, see how many more skills you can check off!

I can:	Before this unit	After this unit
ask and answer questions about what I read.	☐	☐
find the main topic of a text.	☐	☐
find the focus of a paragraph.	☐	☐
tell how one event in history leads to others.	☐	☐
find ways that science ideas go together.	☐	☐
follow steps in directions.	☐	☐

page 14

page 19

page 33

page 47

page 60

page 76

page 80

 Introduction

LAFS.2.RI.1.1 Ask and answer such questions as *who, what, where, when, why,* and *how* to demonstrate understanding of key details in a text.

Lesson 1
Ask and Answer Questions About Key Details

 Learning Target

When you ask questions about what you read, answering those questions helps you understand key details in the text.

▶ Read Asking and answering questions can help you find key details in what you read. **Key details** are important pieces of **information.**

Look carefully at the picture of a bird's nest. What questions could you ask about it?

©Curriculum Associates, LLC Copying is not permitted.

Stay Back, Wolf!

6   Now the porcupette is scared. His muscles tighten. This raises his quills. If the wolf touches the porcupette, the sharp quills will stick into the wolf's skin.

7   The wolf approaches, and the baby porcupine gives two warnings. First, he makes a clacking noise with his teeth. Second, he gives off a strong smell from a small patch of skin on his lower back.

8   The wolf steps back. He has come across quills before and didn't like them. He turns and runs into the forest.

9   *Sniff, sniff.* A new smell floats toward the porcupette. This time it is his mother. They touch nose to nose, and his mother grunts to him.

10   Tired but safe, the porcupette follows his mother. They move through the forest in search of more tasty things to eat.

The mother porcupine and porcupette sit on the log.

▶ **Think** Use what you learned by reading "A Prickly Adventure" to respond to the following questions.

1 This question has two parts. First, answer Part A. Then answer Part B.

Part A
What are a porcupette's favorite foods?

- **A** bark and twigs
- **B** twigs and leaves
- **C** leaves and dandelions
- **D** dandelions and apples

Part B
Write the sentence from the text that gave you the information to answer the question in Part A.

His favorite thing to eat is dandelions

and apples.

2 Read this sentence from the article.

> If the wolf touches the porcupette, the sharp quills will stick into the wolf's skin.

Which question can be answered after reading this sentence?

- **A** How does a porcupette raise its quills?
- **B** Why would a wolf touch a porcupette?
- **C** When might a porcupette use its quills?
- **D** What part of the porcupette has quills?

3 Reread paragraph 3. If you did not know what the word "munches" means, what information from the text helps you learn the meaning?

    A a snap and footsteps

    B sleeps in the hollow

    C his favorite things to eat

    D sniffs in the air

4 Write a *how* question about this article. Then give information from the article that answers the question.

Your question: _How do porcupine straighten the quills._

_____

_____

_____

Information from the article that answers your question:

Their muscles strain and they pull the quills up.

_____

_____

_____

▶ **Write** How does a porcupette protect itself?

5 **Plan Your Response** List key details from the text that tell more about how porcupettes protect themselves.

They make a clamping sound with their teeth and they and he throws of a stench tha got the wolf away.

6 **Short Response** How does a porcupette protect itself? Use the key details you found in the article in your answer.

Hammocks

4 The Native Americans who invented hammocks lived on hot islands. It is easy to keep cool on a hammock.

Lacrosse

5 Have you ever seen people play lacrosse? Native Americans invented this sport. It is played all over the world. Players throw and catch a ball with special sticks.

Kayaks

6 The Native Americans who invented kayaks lived by the water. Kayaks are a great way to travel over water. Today, people love to race kayaks. It is even a sport in the Olympics!

▶ **Think** Use what you learned from reading "Native American Inventions" to answer the following questions.

1 What is paragraph 2 about?

    A types of warm coats

    B where Native Americans live

    C how to invent things

    (D) what a parka is

2 Reread paragraph 4 and look at the picture. Find clues for the meaning of the word "hammock." What is a "hammock"?

    A a sandy beach

    B a straw mat

    (C) a bed hung with ropes

    D a pillow made from leaves

3 What is paragraph 5 **mostly** about?

    A the rules of lacrosse

    (B) what lacrosse is

    C how lacrosse was invented

    D the meaning of the word "lacrosse"

4 Paragraphs 2–6 are like each other in one important way. Which sentence **best** describes how they are alike?

    A   Each describes something made in America.

    B   Each describes a Native American invention.

    C   Each describes something used outdoors.

    D   Each describes how something is made.

5 This question has two parts. First, answer Part A. Then answer Part B.

Part A
Think about what the article tells about kayaks.
What is a "kayak"?

A kyak is a canoe but only for one person.

Part B
Look at the answer you wrote for Part A. Write **two** details from the article that helped you figure out the meaning of the word "kayak."

- Native amercans used canoes so I thought it would be good to write about it.
- a canoe is for two people a kyak is for 1.

Write Based on what you read, what is the main topic of the article?

6 **Plan Your Response** What is the main topic of the article?

    (A)   things that Native Americans invented

    B   where hammocks were first made

    C   how to get maple syrup from a tree

    D   what kayaks have been used for

7 **Short Response** Write about the main topic of "Native American Inventions." Tell what you learned about the topic. Use details from the article in your answer.

The main topic is the inventions that the Native Americans made. I think that their greatest invention was mapel syrup. I think its the greatest because it gives flavor to the food you eat it also can let you experience a good taste.

Learning Target

How does knowing the main topic of a text and the key details of paragraphs help you better understand what you read?

By giving you Some information that you need to Complete things.

 **Introduction**

LAFS.2.RI.1.3 Describe the connection between a series of historical events ... in a text.

Lesson 3
Describing Connections
Between Historical Events

 **Learning Target**

Describing or telling about the connections between historical events in a text will help you understand how and why events in history happen.

▶ **Read** Some texts tell about **historical events,** which are important events that happened in the past. Sometimes these events are **connected.** "To connect" means to fit two or more things together. Events in a history text can follow each other in the order they happened—**first, next,** and **last.** They can also show how one event caused another.

Look at the pictures. Think about how the events are connected.

▶ **Think** Look again at the pictures that show what the girl is doing. How are the events connected? Fill in the chart below to tell how the pictures are connected.

First	Next	Last
The girl is making something.		

▶ **Talk** How are the three pictures connected? Use the pictures to talk about what the girl did first, next, and last. Why did she do it in that order?

◎ **Academic Talk**
Use this phrase and words to talk about the text.
- **historical events** • **first** • **last**
- **connected** • **next**

A New Flag for a New Nation

by Teresa Roberts

1 A long time ago, in the 1700s, the United States was not a country yet. People lived in thirteen colonies. The colonies belonged to England. The people in the colonies wanted to be free. They decided to fight for freedom. The people needed a flag that would stand for all thirteen colonies. General George Washington wanted a flag that everyone would recognize. It would unite the thirteen colonies. Where would this flag come from?

2 One story says that first General George Washington went to see Betsy Ross. She had a sewing shop in Pennsylvania. He asked Betsy Ross if she would make a flag for the thirteen colonies. She said yes. Betsy Ross made a flag with thirteen stars and thirteen stripes. Each star and stripe stood for a colony.

3 The flag that Betsy Ross made was an important symbol in the fight for freedom. It helped the colonists feel proud. Soon, the colonies would become one country. This new flag would stand for the United States of America.

Close Reader Habits

Underline the sentences that tell why Betsy Ross made a flag. Think about how the events are connected.

Shooters

5   The small seeds of jewelweed, witch hazel, and violets grow inside little pods that squeeze them tight. When the time is right, the dry pods pop open—surprise!—and shoot the seeds through the air.

6   Touch one of these seedpods. If it's just-right ripe, watch the seeds fly!

Hitchhikers

7   The seeds of burdock, sticktights, and certain other plants are called burs. Burs have tiny hooks that grab on to the fur of animals that pass by. This free ride may carry the seeds for miles.

8   Have burs come home stuck to you? Or to your dog?

Floaters

9   Water is almost always going somewhere. Seeds that float can bob all the way to a new home. Coconuts are famous for long-distance drifting, but many seeds use water to move.

10   Can you find a seed that floats? Toss it in some water and see if it works as a boat!

Parachuters

11   Some seeds have fine, silky hairs. These hairs can catch a breeze and carry the seeds through the air. Dandelions, milkweeds, and other plants use these "parachutes" to drift.

Think Use what you learned by reading "Seeds Get Around" to respond to the following questions.

1 Look at the types of seeds listed.

floaters ~~burs~~ parachuters ~~shooters~~ ~~nuts~~

Write each type of seed where it belongs in the chart below.

Need Animals to Travel	Use Air or Water to Travel
burs nuts	Parachuters Shooters floaters

2 This question has two parts. First, answer Part A. Then answer Part B.

Part A
How do jewelweed, witch hazel, and violets travel to a new place?

   A   Squirrels bury their seeds and forget them.
   (B) Dry pods shoot their seeds into the air.
   C   The seeds float in the water of a stream.
   D   Their hairs help them fly in the breeze.

Part B
Write the sentence from the passage that helped you answer the question in Part A.

Jewelweed, witch hazel and violets

3 Why can some seeds called burs stick to the fur of animals?

    A Burs have tiny hooks.

    B Burs have a sticky glue.

    C Burs have magnets.

    D Burs have arms.

4 Write the base word for each of these words from the selection.

    A collecting   _____

    B buried, burying   _____

    C drifting   _____

    D planted   _____

5 How are all of the seeds in this article alike?

    A They can all fly through the air.

    B They can all stick to other things.

    C They can all travel from place to place.

    D They can all float down a river.

▶ ✏️ **Write** How are burs and parachuting seeds different from other seeds?

6 **Plan Your Response** Identify the special parts of burs and parachuting seeds.

_____

_____

_____

_____

_____

7 **Short Response** How are burs and parachuting seeds different from other seeds? Use details from the article in your answer.

_____

_____

_____

_____

_____

_____

Learning Target

How does describing how ideas in science texts are connected help you understand how things work and why things change?

_____

_____

_____

_____

LAFS.2.RI.1.3 Describe the connection between … steps in technical procedures in a text.

Lesson 5
Describing Connections Between Steps

 **Learning Target**

Looking at how steps in a process are connected will help you understand what you read.

▶ **Read** Directions are a set of **steps in a process** that tell you how to make or do something. Sometimes, numbers show the **order** of the steps. Other times, words such as **first, next, then,** and **last** are clues that let you know the order.

Look at these pictures. The pictures show the steps of a science experiment. Are these steps in the right order? How do you know?

Watch as the sun melts the ice.

Fill a glass with ice cubes.

Set the glass in a warm, sunny area.

▶ **Think** Look back at the pictures to figure out what happens first, next, and last. Then write the steps in the right order to fill in the chart.

Step	Directions
1	**First,** fill a glass with ice cubes.
2	**Next,**
3	**Last,**

▶ **Talk** Why is the order of the steps important? What would happen if you did Step 2 before Step 1?

◎ **Academic Talk**
Use these words to talk about the text.
- **steps in a process**
- **next**
- **order**
- **then**
- **first**
- **last**

START A  WEATHER WALL

What You Need

- Pictures of different kinds of weather

- Tape

- A wall

What You Do

First, tape the picture on the wall that best matches the weather outside. Next, if you think the weather will change later in the day, tape another picture on the wall that best matches your guess. Last, check both pictures at the end of the day to see if you guessed correctly. Make a note!

> **Close Reader Habits**
>
> **Underline** what you should do first. **Circle** the clues that tell you the order for the rest of the steps.

Explore **How do you know what steps to follow in directions and when to do them?**

> I wonder what these directions tell me to do. I'll read all the directions. Then I will follow the steps.

▶ **Think**

1 Look back at the directions for the weather wall. Fill in the steps in the chart, in the right order. Begin each sentence with one of these words: *first, next, last.*

Step	Directions
1	
2	
3	

▶ **Talk**

2 What would happen if you skipped step 2? Talk with your partner about why step 2 is important.

▶ **Write**

3 **Short Response** What words help you know the order of the steps in the directions? Write about how the words help. Write your answer in the space on page 72.

> HINT Think about the order in which things happen.

> **Read**

Which Way Does the Wind Blow?

by Stephen Krensky

Do you know which direction the wind blows where you live? You can make a wind streamer to find out.

What You Do

1. First, tear off several four-foot-long pieces from a roll of crepe paper.

2. Next, pull one end of a piece of paper through the plastic ring until the two ends meet.

3. Then tie the crepe paper in a knot at the ring. Repeat steps 2 and 3 for the other pieces of paper. Now you have a wind streamer.

4. Last, tape the wind streamer to a tree branch or a pole. Make sure the air can reach the crepe paper from any direction.

Use the compass to see in what direction the crepe paper blows. Does the direction change? Does it always blow in the same direction? Write what you see.

WHAT YOU NEED

- **crepe paper**
- **plastic ring**
- **tape**
- **compass**

Close Reader Habits

How will you find out which way the wind blows? Reread the last paragraph and **underline** the sentence that tells you.

Think

1 What do these directions tell you how to do? Write your answer.

_____

_____

_____

_____

> Reread the directions, and think about what happens in each step. Look for the clues that tell you the order of the steps.

2 What should you do after you tie all the crepe paper to the plastic ring?

A Tear off three long pieces from a roll of crepe paper.

B Make sure the ends of the crepe paper are even.

C Tape the wind streamer to a tree branch or pole.

D Use a compass to find a tree branch.

Talk

3 Explain how the picture helps you follow steps 2 and 3.

Write

4 **Short Response** How will following the steps in a process help you know which way the wind blows? Write your answer in the space on page 73.

> **HINT** Think about what you make when you follow the steps.

▶ **Write** **Use the space below to write your answer to the question on page 69.**

START A WEATHER WALL ☀️ 🌨️ ☂️ 🌬️

3 **Short Response** What words help you know the order of the steps in the directions? Write about how the words help.

> **HINT** Think about the order in which things happen.

_____

_____

_____

_____

_____

_____

Don't forget to check your writing.

Write Use the space below to write your answer to the question on page 71.

Which Way Does the Wind Blow?

4 **Short Response** How will following the steps in a process help you know which way the wind blows?

> **HINT** Think about what you make when you follow the steps.

_____

_____

_____

_____

_____

_____

Check Your Writing

☐ Did you read the question carefully?

☐ Can you say the question in your own words?

☐ Did you use proof from the text in your answer?

☐ Are your ideas in a good, clear order?

☐ Did you answer in full sentences?

☐ Did you check your spelling, capital letters, and periods?

WORDS TO KNOW
As you read, look inside, around, and beyond these words to figure out what they mean.

- **shallow**
- **mirror**
- **refraction**

How Do You Make a Rainbow?

by Shar Levine and Leslie Johnstone

Where do rainbows come from?

If the sun shines right after a rain, look and you may be lucky enough to see a rainbow. But you don't need to wait for rain to see a rainbow. You can make your own.

You need

a sunny day **a mirror** **adult helper**

shallow glass baking dish **water** **white paper or cardboard**

Do This

1 Put the glass baking dish flat on the ground or on a table.

2 Place the mirror in the dish. Lean it up against one side.

3 Turn the dish so the mirror faces the sun.

4 Add water until the dish is about half full.

5 Ask your helper to hold up the paper at the end of the dish away from the mirror and move it around slowly. Watch for the sunlight bouncing off the mirror.

What happened?

A rainbow appeared! The water in the dish bent the sunlight. Even though sunlight looks white, it has colors in it. And when the light is bent, it breaks up into red, orange, yellow, green, blue, indigo (a purplish color), and violet. This is called **refraction.** It's how white sunlight puts a rainbow on the paper.

After a rain, lots of small drops are still in the air. When sunlight hits the drops, the light bends to make a rainbow, just like the rainbow you made.

▶ **Think** Use what you learned by reading "How Do You Make a Rainbow?" to respond to the following questions.

1 Put the steps for making a rainbow in the order you should do them. Write the numbers 1 to 5 on the line before each sentence.

_____4_____ Add water to the dish.

_____5_____ Hold up the paper and move it around slowly.

_____1_____ Put the dish on the ground or on a table.

_____3_____ Turn the dish so the mirror faces the sun.

_____2_____ Place the mirror in the dish.

2 This question has two parts. First, answer Part A. Then answer Part B.

Part A
What should happen before the dish is turned to face the sun?

(A) The mirror should be placed in the dish.

B Water should be added to the dish.

C The helper should hold up the paper.

D Sunlight should bounce off the mirror.

Part B
Write the step from the text that helped you answer the question in Part A.

Place the mirror in the dish.

3 How does the picture by step 2 help you understand what to do?

    A It shows where to place the mirror in the dish.

    B It shows how to make the sunlight bounce off the mirror.

    C It shows how to turn the dish so that it faces the sun.

    D It shows where your adult helper should stand.

4 What would happen if you did step 5 before step 4?

    A The paper would not stay up.

    B Sunlight would not shine on the mirror.

    C The rainbow would not appear.

    D The rainbow would have fewer colors.

5 Based on clues in the text, what does the word "appeared" mean in this sentence?

    A rainbow appeared! The water in the dish bent the sunlight.

    A hid the light

    B went missing

    C could be seen

    D became very big

▶ **Write** What are the steps in the directions?

6 **Plan Your Response** Make a list of the steps in the directions. Think about how the steps help you understand how rainbows are formed.

7 **Short Response** How does following these directions help you understand how real rainbows are formed?

Rain gets hit by sunlight and acts like a mirror and then it shows a rainbow.

Learning Target

Now you know directions are a set of steps that tell you how to make or do something. Why is it important to follow the steps in the order they are written?

Because if you don't you won't get a rainbow

Read the science article. Then answer the questions that follow.

Making an Indoor Garden

by Rashida Darcy

1   If you look closely at the word "terrarium," you can see the word part "terra" at the beginning. "Terra" means "earth." So what's a terrarium? It's a container of soil that plants can live in.

2   Terrariums come in all shapes and sizes. They can as big as a table and reach the ceiling. Or they can be as small as a fishbowl and fit on a shelf.

3   A terrarium is a piece of nature. You can keep it in your kitchen or bedroom. Like a garden, it can include rocks and sticks. Even frogs or snakes may live inside.

4   You can build your own terrarium with help from an adult. Here's one way to do it.

You will need:

- a clean, empty 1-gallon water jug
- tape
- soil
- pebbles
- 2 plants

Do This

1. Have an adult help you carefully cut off the top of the water jug. Put tape over the edge to cover up sharp corners.

2. Next, put some pebbles on the bottom of the container.

3. Cover the pebbles with about two inches of soil.

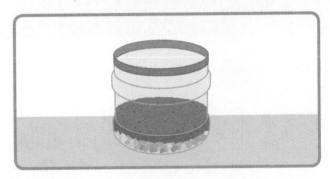

4. Dig two small holes in the soil.

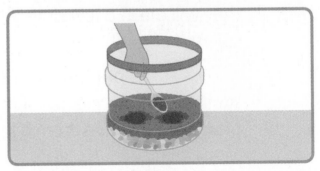

5. Put one plant in each hole. Then shape the soil so it holds the plant in place.

6. Put the top back on.

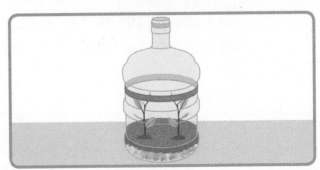

Terrariums are a fun way to grow a garden inside your home.

5   You've just made a terrarium! But now you need to take care of it. If you don't care for the plants, they will die in a few days. Plants need soil to live, but soil isn't enough. They also need air, light, and water.

6   So put the terrarium in a place that gets sunshine. Leave the top of the terrarium open so the plants get air. Give them a little water every day.

7   Before long, you'll probably notice that your plants are growing . . . and growing . . . and growing some more. You're growing a garden!

▶ Think

1 This question has two parts. First, answer Part A. Then answer Part B.

Part A
What is the main topic of this article?

    A   how to build a terrarium

    B   what plants need to live

    C   which plants grow indoors

    D   why people have gardens

Part B
Write **one** sentence from the article that helped you answer the question in Part A.

_____

_____

_____

2 How does the picture that goes with step 3 help you understand what to do?

    A   It shows how to dig holes in the soil.

    B   It shows how much soil to put in the jug.

    C   It shows how to cut the top off the jug.

    D   It shows how to shape the soil to hold the plants.

3 Put the steps for making a terrarium in the order you should do them.
Write the numbers 1 to 4 on the line before each sentence.

_____ Dig two small holes in the soil.

_____ Put some pebbles on the bottom of the container.

_____ Cut off the top of the water jug.

_____ Cover the pebbles with two inches of soil.

4 Why should you leave the top of the terrarium open?

    A   to let in sunshine

    B   to let in air

    C   to let in rain

    D   to let in frogs

5 What is paragraph 6 **mostly** about?

    A   what kinds plants to put in a terrarium

    B   when to water plants in a terrarium

    C   how to take care of plants in a terrarium

    D   why plants need soil and water to live

6 Write a *what* question about this article. Then give information from the article that answers the question.

Your question:

_____

_____

_____

_____

Information from the article that answers your question:

_____

_____

_____

_____

_____

▶ **Read**

Read the history article. Then answer the questions that follow.

Owney

The Dog Who Rode the Trains

by S. W. James

1   One night in 1888, a cold, black nose poked into the room. Then a scruffy brown dog walked into the post office in Albany, New York.

2   The mail workers were too busy to see the brown dog. They sorted the mail and put it in big bags. Later, those mailbags would be put on trains and taken to other places.

3   The brown dog sniffed at the mailbags. He wagged his scruffy tail. Then he curled up on a bag and fell asleep.

4   All the mail workers liked the dog. Soon, they named him Owney. They fed him and played with him. Best of all, they let Owney ride on the wagons with the mailbags. Owney made the Albany post office his home.

5   One day, Owney hopped onto a train with the mailbags. Owney went for a ride. And he loved it! After that, Owney rode trains all over the United States. He went to Canada and Mexico, too. Once, Owney even traveled around the world! But Owney always came home.

6   At each stop, Owney made new friends. Owney became famous! His new friends gave Owney special tags. The tags told everyone where Owney had visited. Owney's tags jingled as he walked.

7   Today, you can see Owney and his tags in a museum. The post office made a stamp with his picture on it. Now, like Owney, his picture travels with the mail!

Owney with his special tags

▶ Think

7 What is paragraph 5 **mostly** about?

    A   how Owney got his name

    B   why Owney always came back home

    C   when Owney first came to the post office

    D   where Owney traveled

8 Which question can be answered by reading paragraph 7?

    A   When did Owney first go into a post office?

    B   What places did Owney visit?

    C   Why did Owney like to travel on trains?

    D   Where can you see Owney's tags today?

9 This question has two parts. First, answer Part A. Then answer Part B.

Part A

Read the sentence from the article.

> **Then a <u>scruffy</u> brown dog with muddy paws and fur sticking out walked into the post office in Albany, New York.**

Based on clues in the text, what does the word "scruffy" mean?

    A   messy

    B   scary

    C   large

    D   friendly

Part B

Circle words in the sentence in Part A that help you figure out what "scruffy" means.

10 Write a *how* question about this article. Then give information from the article that answers the question.

Your question:

How did owney become famous?

Information from the article that answers your question:

By traveling around the world.

11 This question has two parts. First, answer Part A. Then answer Part B.

Part A

Why did the post office put Owney's picture on a stamp?

(A) Owney traveled to many places with the mail.

B Owney liked to sleep on mailbags.

C Owney was owned by a mail worker.

D Owney once hopped onto a train.

Part B

Underline the sentence in paragraph 7 that tells about the answer to Part A.

　Today, you can see Owney and his tags in a museum.
The post office made a stamp with his picture on it.
Now, like Owney, his picture travels with the mail!

 **Write**

Extended Response How did Owney become famous?

12 **Plan Your Response** Fill in the chart with key details from the article that tell how Owney became a famous dog.

How Owney Made a Post Office His Home	He went in and fell asleep on one of the mail bags.
Why Owney Was Able to Travel All Over the United States	He was able to do that because he hopped on a train.
What Happened to Owney on His Trips	He made new friends wherever he went.

13 **Write an Extended Response** How did Owney became a famous dog?
Use the details you found in the article in your answer.

He traveled many places and made new friends. on every thip he made he got a badge. soon he traveled all over the world and the friends gave him the badges So he could remember each and every one of them

Unit 2

Key Ideas and Details in Literature

What are some of your favorite stories? Do you like funny stories? Do you like stories with lots of adventure? Or maybe you like fairy tales, such as "Hansel and Gretel."

In this unit, you will read different kinds of stories. In all of them, you can ask questions about what the characters say and do. You'll learn how some stories can teach lessons about life. And you'll learn how to retell stories in your own words. When you ask questions about what happens and why, you'll have more fun reading and telling stories.

✓ Self Check

Before starting this unit, check off the skills you know below. As you complete each lesson, see how many more skills you can check off!

I can:	Before this unit	After this unit
ask and answer questions about a story.	☐	☐
tell what happens in a story in my own words.	☐	☐
describe the lesson the story characters learn.	☐	☐
tell how characters deal with their problems.	☐	☐

page 101

page 114

page 122

page 128

page 143

page 152

 **Introduction**

LAFS.2.RL.1.1 Ask and answer such questions as *who, what, where, when, why,* and how to demonstrate understanding of key details in a text.

Lesson 6
Ask and Answer Questions About Stories

When you ask questions about what you read, answering those questions will help you understand the key details in a story.

▶ **Read** Asking questions as you read will help you find and understand key details. **Key details** are important pieces of information, like who and what the story is about. Answering questions can also help you show what you know about the story.

Look carefully at this cartoon. What questions could you ask about it?

Maria and Pete went for a hike with Mom and Dad.

They came to a wide river.

How will we get across?

▶ **Think** What are some questions you could ask and answer about the story in the cartoon? In the chart, write three more questions about the story and your answers. Good questions often begin with the words *who, what, where, when, why,* or *how.*

Ask Questions	Answer Questions
Who is in the story?	Maria, Pete, Mom, and Dad
What do they do?	They are on a hike.

▶ **Talk** Think about what has happened so far. Ask your partner a question about something else that might happen in the story. Discuss your answers.

 **Academic Talk**
Use this phrase to talk about the text.
• **key details**

> Read

SAVING the TRAIN

by Annika Pedersen

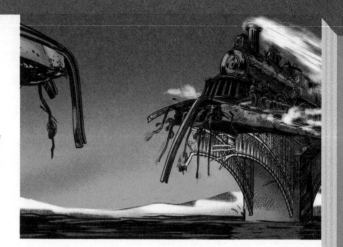

1   Owen and Amy walked along the Green River. They had never seen the water so high. A storm the day before had brought heavy rain. As they walked around a bend in the river, they could hardly believe their eyes. The railroad bridge over the river had fallen into the rushing water!

2   "The noon train will be here soon!" Owen said to his sister. "It'll crash right into the river. We've got to go tell someone!"

3   "There's no time to get anyone," Amy said. "We'll have to stop it ourselves. I have an idea!" she shouted, as she turned and sped home.

4   When she got there, Amy took a big white tablecloth from the table. She grabbed a can of red paint and a brush. Then she painted the words "STOP! BRIDGE OUT!" on the cloth.

5   Amy dashed as fast as she could back to Owen. They could hear the train coming! They held the painted cloth between them and waved. But the train flew by. Had no one seen their warning?

6   A second later the train's brakes screeched, and its whistle blew loudly. It came to a full stop. Amy and Owen had saved the train!

Close Reader Habits

Underline key details about important parts of the story. These are details that answer *who, what, when, where,* and *why* questions.

Explore   **What questions can you ask and answer about the key details of the story?**

> I will ask questions to help me as I read. I can ask who, what, where, why, or how.

▶ Think

1 Write questions in the chart. Reread the story to find the answers. Write the answers in the chart.

Ask Questions	Answer Questions

▶ Talk

2 Think of another question about a key detail in the story. Find and underline the answer in the story. Ask your partner the question and discuss the answer.

Write

3 **Short Response** Why does Amy make the warning sign? What happens in the first part of the story that helps you answer this question? Write your answer in the space on page 98.

> **HINT** Reread the first part of the story before you write your answer.

The CLIMB

by Wendell Riley

1   "Grandpa, look!" I cried. "It's a ship!" I could hardly believe my eyes. There was a huge ship with tall sails, far out at sea. We waved our arms and shouted, "Help! Help!"

2   We had been stranded on the island for weeks. I was out fishing with Grandpa one day when the weather suddenly changed. A storm blew our fishing boat off course and onto a rocky island. Grandpa steered the best he could, landing us on the shore. But our boat was ruined. We had no way back to the little seaside town we called home.

3   The huge ship was the first we'd seen—and it was sailing right past us! "It's no use, Sara," Grandpa said. "They can't see us."

4   "But they could if I was up there," I said. I pointed to the top of a high, rocky hill. Grandpa looked worried, but he knew there was no other way. I had to climb the rocks quickly but carefully—and not look down! When I got to the top, I shouted, and flashed a small mirror. I was about to give up, when a light flashed back. We were saved!

Close Reader Habits

What questions can you ask about the story? **Underline** the details that help you answer your questions.

Think

1 Where does the story take place?

> **A** on a huge ship at sea
>
> **B** on Grandpa's fishing boat
>
> **C** on a small rocky island
>
> **D** in a little seaside town

I'm going to reread the story carefully and look for details that tell who, where, what, and why.

2 What causes Sara and Grandpa's fishing boat to crash? Choose the sentence from the story that answers this question.

> **A** "We had been stranded on the island for weeks."
>
> **B** "A storm blew our fishing boat off course and onto a rocky island."
>
> **C** "We had no way back to the little seaside town we called home."
>
> **D** "When I got to the top, I shouted, and flashed a small mirror."

Talk

3 Think of a *how* or *why* question about the story. Ask your partner the question. Together, find the answer in the story and discuss why it is important.

 ## Write

4 **Short Response** Read this sentence from the story.

> **I was about to give up, when a light flashed back.**

Write a question that the sentence could answer. Then choose another sentence and write a question for that sentence. Write your answer in the space on page 99.

HINT Review the sentence in the story to use to write the question.

Write **Use the space below to write your answer to the question on page 95.**

SAVING *the* TRAIN

3 **Short Response** Why does Amy make the warning sign? What happens in the first part of the story that helps you answer this question?

> **HINT** Reread the first part of the story before you write your answer.

Don't forget to check your writing.

©Curriculum Associates, LLC   Copying is not permitted.

4   The wolf trotted into the meadow wearing the fleece. He walked among the sheep. And this time, the shepherd didn't chase him away.

5   That very night, the wolf carried off a large sheep to have for his dinner.

6   The next day, the wolf wore the fleece again and strolled freely among the sheep. But this time, the shepherd did notice the wolf. He said to himself, "That looks like a fine sheep for my stew tonight."

7   Before the wolf could leap away, the shepherd grabbed him. And that night, the shepherd enjoyed a delicious stew.

▶ **Think** Use what you learned by reading "The Wolf in Sheep's Clothing" to respond to the following questions.

1 Read this sentence from the story.

> **Every time he saw the wolf, he chased him back into the forest.**

Why is this event important to the beginning of the story?

   A It tells why the wolf can't get near the sheep.

   B It tells why the sheep are not afraid of the wolf.

   C It tells why the wolf wanted to eat the sheep.

   D It tells why the shepherd forgot the fleece.

2 This question has two parts. First, answer Part A. Then answer Part B.

Part A
How did the wolf fool the shepherd?

   A He made a noise like a sheep.

   B He hid in the forest.

   C He waited until the shepherd left.

   D He wore the fleece of a sheep.

Part B
Write the sentence from the text that explains why the wolf's trick worked.

_____

_____

_____

_____

3 Look at the chart. It tells the order of some of the events in the story.

1	2	3
The wolf puts on a sheep's fluffy, white fleece.		The wolf carries off a sheep for his dinner.

Which sentence belongs in the empty box?

A The shepherd chases the wolf into the forest.

B The wolf walks into the herd of sheep.

C The shepherd notices the wolf.

D The shepherd cooks a delicious stew.

4 Which choice **best** shows what "strolled" means in the following sentence?

The next day, the wolf wore the fleece again and strolled freely among the sheep.

A He ran through the herd of sheep.

B He walked slowly among the sheep.

C He stayed away from the sheep.

D He chased the sheep in the meadow.

Write What happens in this story?

5 **Plan Your Response** List important events from the beginning, middle, and end of the story.

_____

_____

_____

_____

_____

_____

6 **Short Response** Recount the whole story. Be sure to use your own words. Tell what happens at the beginning, middle, and end of the story. Use the events from your list.

_____

_____

_____

_____

_____

_____

_____

_____

_____

 ## Learning Target

**Now you know how to recount a story. Why is it important
to tell the important events in order?**

_____

_____

_____

Lesson 8
Determining the Central Message

Learning Target

Knowing which events are most important in a story will help you figure out the story's lesson or central message.

▶ Read The **central message** of a story is the big idea or **lesson** the story teaches. Important events in a story help you figure out the central message.

Look at the cartoon. Think about a lesson that it teaches.

Come play with us.

▶ **Think** The events in the cartoon tell a story. In the chart below, answer the questions to tell about the most important event in each picture.

What Are the Most Important Events?

First picture Why does the boy look sad?	
Second picture What does the girl say to the boy?	
Third picture What is the boy doing?	

▶ **Talk** What lesson do you think the events in the cartoon teach? Use the chart above and the cartoon to talk about the lesson the cartoon teaches.

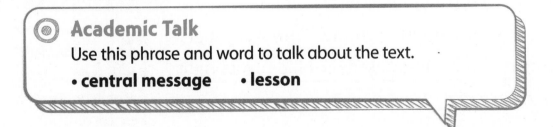

Academic Talk
Use this phrase and word to talk about the text.
- **central message**
- **lesson**

The Blue Coyote

from a Native American fable

1 Long ago, there lived a hungry coyote. One day, he found a juicy bone! He grabbed it and ran away.

2 When he jumped over a fence, he landed in a big tub filled with blue ink. Now his fur was bright blue!

3 The coyote went to the forest. The animals had never seen such a strange blue creature. They were scared and ran away. The sneaky coyote thought of a plan to make the animals give him all the food he wanted.

4 He told the animals he was their new king. They believed him! They also brought him all the food he wanted.

5 One night, he heard coyotes howling at the moon. He could not stop himself. He started howling, too!

6 When the other animals heard him, they knew he was really just another coyote. They were angry at being tricked! They chased the blue coyote right out of the woods.

Close Reader Habits

Underline words or sentences that tell why the animals become angry at the blue coyote.

Explore How do the events in the story help you figure out its central message?

I wonder what lesson the coyote learns. I'll find the most important events in the story.

▶ **Think**

1 Answer the questions in the chart to tell about the most important events in the story.

What Are the Most Important Events?

How does the blue coyote become blue?	
Why do the animals bring the blue coyote food?	
Why does the blue coyote start howling?	

▶ **Talk**

2 What happens after the animals hear the blue coyote howling? Talk about the answer with your partner.

HINT Think about how the animals feel about the trick the blue coyote has played on them.

 ▶ **Write**

3 **Short Response** What lesson do you think the blue coyote learns? Write about an event from the story to explain your answer. Write your answer in the space on page 126.

The Boy Who Cried Wolf

an Aesop fable

1   Long ago, a boy sat watching a farmer's sheep. He was bored, so he decided to play a trick. "Wolf! Wolf!" he shouted. "A wolf is chasing the sheep!"

2   The villagers came running, but instead of a wolf, they found the boy laughing. "There really isn't any wolf! I just wanted to fool you," he said.

3   The angry villagers returned to the village.

4   However, the boy quickly grew bored again. "Wolf!" he shouted. "A wolf is chasing the sheep!"

5   Again, the villagers came running, and they were furious to find that the boy had tricked them a second time.

6   At the end of the day, the boy saw a real wolf. "Wolf!" he shouted. "There's a wolf after the sheep!" But no one came, and the boy ran to the village crying.

7   "There was a wolf, and no one came!" he said.

"We didn't believe you," the villagers said. "No one believes a liar, even when he tells the truth."

Close Reader Habits

Which events help you figure out the central message of the story? **Underline** words and sentences that tell what the villagers do each time the boy cries "Wolf!"

Think

1 Why does the boy shout "Wolf!" the first time?

    A He thinks he sees a wolf chasing the sheep.

    B He hopes he can get a real wolf to come.

    C He wants to play a joke on the villagers.

    D He feels afraid watching the sheep by himself.

> Rereading the story will help you figure out the lesson the character learns.

2 What do the villagers do when the boy shouts "Wolf!" the second time?

    A They get angry at the boy for tricking them again.

    B They laugh at being fooled twice by the boy's trick.

    C They look all over for a wolf but cannot find it.

    D They don't come because they don't believe him.

Talk

3 Reread the story. Why don't the villagers believe the boy at the end? Talk about the answer with your partner and look at the important events you underlined in the story.

Write

4 **Short Response** Use details from the story to answer the question below. Write your answer in the space on page 127.

What is the central message of the story?

> **HINT** Look for the important event that happens at the end of the story.

Write Use the space below to write your answer to the question on page 123.

The Blue Coyote

3 **Short Response** What lesson do you think the blue coyote learns? Write about an event from the story to explain your answer.

_____

_____

_____

_____

_____

_____

Don't forget to check your writing.

Write Use the space below to write your answer to the question on page 125.

The Boy Who Cried **Wolf**

4 **Short Response** Use details from the story to answer the question below.

What is the central message of the story?

> **HINT** Look for the important event that happens at the end of the story.

_____

_____

_____

_____

_____

Check Your Writing

☐ Did you read the question carefully?

☐ Can you say the question in your own words?

☐ Did you use proof from the text in your answer?

☐ Are your ideas in a good, clear order?

☐ Did you answer in full sentences?

☐ Did you check your spelling, capital letters, and periods?

▶ **Read**

The Monkey and the Peas

a folktale from India

> **WORDS TO KNOW**
>
> As you read, look inside, around, and beyond these words to figure out what they mean.
>
> • **sights**
>
> • **gain**

1   Once upon a time, there was a king who loved to travel. But he didn't like to visit places in his own country. He thought that more beautiful sights could only be seen in other lands.

2   One day, the king and his army were riding their horses through another strange new land. When they became tired, they set up a camp to rest. The horses were hungry, so the soldiers fed them peas.

3   A monkey who lived in the forest was watching the king's men from a high tree. He saw the horses eating peas. So he jumped down from the tree to get some of the peas for his dinner.

4   He quickly filled his mouth and hands with peas. Then he climbed back up the tree. There he sat down to eat the peas.

5   As he ate the peas, one pea fell from his hand to the ground. The monkey dropped all the peas he had in his hands. He ran down to look for the lost pea.

6   The monkey could not find the one lost pea. The other peas the monkey had dropped rolled away. He climbed up the tree again and lay on its trunk, looking sad. The monkey was very disappointed.

7   The king was watching the monkey from the camp. He said to himself, "To get one pea, that monkey threw away the rest. I would not be like this foolish monkey. He lost everything while trying to gain so little. I will go back to my own country. I will enjoy what I already have."

8   So the king and his army rode back to their country. The king found many beautiful sights in his own land.

Think Use what you learned from reading "The Monkey and the Peas" to answer the following questions.

1 This question has two parts. First, answer Part A. Then answer Part B.

Part A
Why does the king visit another country at the beginning of the story?

(A) to find more beautiful sights in other lands

B to make sure his soldiers and his horses are safe

C to see monkeys in his own country

D to be king of more than one country

Part B
Write the sentence from the story that helped you answer the question in Part A.

He thought that more beautiful sights could only be seen in other lands

2 Read the following sentences from paragraph 7 of the story.

I would not be like this <u>foolish</u> monkey. He lost everything while trying to gain so little.

What does the word "foolish" mean in the sentence?

A helpful

B clumsy

C silly

(D) careless

3 Read paragraph 6 of the story.

The monkey could not find the one lost pea. The other peas the monkey had dropped rolled away. He climbed up the tree again and lay on its trunk, looking sad. The monkey was very <u>disappointed</u>.

Circle the word in paragraph 6 that **best** helps you know what "disappointed" means.

4 Which event from the story is **most** important to understanding the central message?

   A   The king rides his horse through a new land.

   B   The soldiers give the horses peas to eat.

   C   The monkey watches the king's men from a high tree.

   D   The monkey drops all the peas to look for the lost one.

5 Which sentence from the story **best** tells why the king goes back to his own country after watching the monkey?

   A   "As he ate the peas, one pea fell from his hand to the ground."

   B   "The monkey could not find the one lost pea."

   C   "The other peas the monkey had dropped rolled away."

   D   "He lost everything while trying to gain so little."

▶ **Write** What is the central message of the story?

6 **Plan Your Response** Answer the questions in the chart to tell about the most important events in the story.

Important Events in "The Monkey and the Peas"

Why does the monkey climb down the tree the first time?	To get the peas
Why does the monkey climb down from the tree the second time?	to recover the lost pea
What does the king think about the monkey?	He lost a lot trying to get so little
Why does the king go back to his own country?	because he did not want to be like the monkey

7 **Short Response** The king learns an important lesson from watching the monkey. What is this lesson or central message of the story? Use information from the chart above in your answer.

_____

_____

_____

_____

_____

_____

_____

_____

_____

Learning Target

How do the important events in a story help you figure out its central message or lesson?

_____

_____

_____

_____

LAFS.2.RL.1.3 Describe how characters in a story respond to major events and challenges.

Lesson 9
Describing How Characters Act

Learning Target

Describing how characters in a story respond to important events and challenges will help you understand how and why they act the way they do.

▶ **Read** **Characters** are the people or animals in a story that face a **challenge.** A challenge is a problem that needs to be solved. Describing how characters **respond** to challenges will help you get to know them better.

Look at the picture. What is the challenge? How does each character respond? Think about why each boy acts that way.

▶ **Think**   Complete the chart. Tell what the challenge is. Then tell how each character responds to it.

What the Challenge Is	How the Characters Respond
	• Little boy
	• Older boy

▶ **Talk**   What will make the little boy happy? Use what you see in the picture to answer.

◎ **Academic Talk**
Use these words to talk about the text.
- **characters**   • **respond**   • **challenge**

▶ **Read**

A Puppy for Oscar

by Jane Lawrence

1 Oscar wanted a puppy more than anything in the world. But his mom kept saying they could not have a dog in their apartment.

2 "We do not have a yard," she said. "And a dog needs space to run."

3 Oscar had an idea. There was a city park very close to their apartment. The park was really big. Maybe part of it could be turned into a park for dogs. Then Oscar's puppy would have a place to run!

4 Now Oscar needed to turn his idea into a plan. Oscar worked very hard. He wrote letters to newspapers. He wrote to the mayor about his idea for a dog park. He talked to people about his idea. Then he got many of them to sign their names to a letter saying they wanted a dog park, too.

5 It took over a year, but Oscar finally got his dog park. And then he got what he really wanted—a new puppy!

Close Reader Habits

Circle a sentence that tells what Oscar's challenge is.
Underline a sentence that tells how he responds to the challenge.

Explore What is the challenge in this story, and how does Oscar respond to it?

Think

Rereading the story will help you figure out how Oscar responds to his challenge.

1 Complete the chart to help you understand Oscar's challenge and how he responds to the challenge.

Oscar's Challenge	How Oscar Responds to the Challenge

Talk

2 What is the main thing Oscar does to respond to his challenge? Describe an event from the story to explain your answer.

Write

3 **Short Response** What do Oscar's actions tell you about him? Use an event from the story to explain your answer. Write your answer in the space on page 140.

HINT What does Oscar do? Make a list of the things he does in the story.

The Snowstorm

by Annika Pedersen

1   The wind blew hard, shaking the barn. Outside, the falling snow whipped this way and that. Inside, Greta and her mother counted the sheep they had just brought down from the mountain. One of the sheep was missing, but which one? They saw that Lizzie, one of the new lambs, had been left behind.

2   Greta and her mother started back up the mountain to look for her, but there wasn't much time. Already, they could hardly see a thing in the heavy, blowing snow. "Lizzie! Lizzie!" they called out.

3   At last, they heard her crying back *baa-aa-aa!* They had found Lizzie, but now they were lost. How would they find their way home? Their whole world had gone white!

4   Then Greta saw a stream nearby. The blinding snow was still melting in it! She and her mother could follow the stream's twisting dark line down the mountain. It would lead them back to the gate near their barn.

5   Greta held the little lamb tight. Soon, everyone would be safe at home.

Close Reader Habits

What problem do Greta and her mom have *after* they find Lizzie? **Underline** two sentences that tell you what challenge they face.

▶ **Think**

1 Why is finding the lost lamb a challenge for Greta and her mother?

Rereading the story will help you figure out how the characters face a challenge.

A They are not really sure the lamb is still missing.

B They know they will be in great danger from the storm.

C They have already climbed the mountain once and are worn out.

D They are afraid to leave the sheep alone in the barn.

2 Which **best** tells about the challenge that Greta and her mother must face after they find Lizzie?

A They can't get Lizzie to stop crying *baa-aa-aa*.

B They are getting very cold from the wind and snow.

C They have to make sure there aren't any other lost sheep.

D They can't see how to get back home in the snowstorm.

▶ **Talk**

3 What do Greta and her mom do to respond to the challenge of finding the lost sheep? Tell your partner.

▶ **Write**

4 **Short Response** Tell what Greta sees in the storm and how it will help her, her mother, and Lizzie get home. Write your answer in the space on page 141.

HINT Think about how Greta responds to the new challenge they face.

Write **Use the space below to write your answer to the question on page 137.**

A Puppy for Oscar

3 **Short Response** What do Oscar's actions tell you about him? Use an event from the story to explain your answer.

> **HINT** What does Oscar do? Make a list of the things he does in the story.

_____

_____

_____

_____

_____

_____

_____

> Don't forget to check your writing.

page 160

page 168

page 182

page 190

page 197

page 210

page 220

Lesson 10
Unfamiliar Words

Learning Target

Figuring out the meanings of important words in a text will help you better understand the topic.

▶ **Read** Readers have many ways to figure out a new word. One way is to look for **clues** in the words and **phrases** around the new word. You can also ask yourself what you may already know about the **subject** or topic.

Look at the photo and read the sentences below it. Then find clues about the meaning of the word "extinguish."

Firefighters work together to extinguish a fire.
After they put out the fire, they search for hot spots.

▶ **Think** Use the chart to write the clues in the picture for the word "extinguish." Write the word on the top line. Write the clues. Then write what you think the word means.

Word:	
What is a clue from the sentences?	The second sentence says "they put out
What is a clue from the picture?	
What does the word "extinguish" mean?	

▶ **Talk** Look at the picture again. Talk to your partner about what a firefighter does to extinguish a fire.

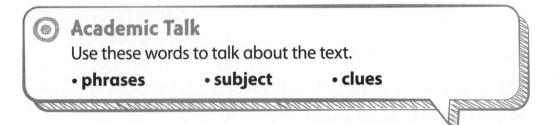

◎ **Academic Talk**
Use these words to talk about the text.
- **phrases**   - **subject**   - **clues**

Taking Flight on a
Jumbo Jet

by Kathryn Thomas

1   Airplanes carry people all over the world. Flying safely from place to place is a big job. It takes a whole team of people to do it. The team is called an aircrew. It is headed by a captain.

2   The captain of an airplane is also the pilot. The pilot controls how high and fast the plane flies. The first officer is the co-pilot. That person takes over if the captain needs to rest. There is also a flight engineer who controls the engines to make sure everything is working.

3   Passengers ride in the cabin of the plane. The cabin crew is made up of flight attendants. Their main job is to help passengers travel safely. They show passengers what to do if there is trouble with the plane. They help passengers store their baggage. They also serve passengers food and drinks.

4   Aircrews take people on thousands of flights each day. Though passengers may not notice, the crews are always hard at work.

Close Reader Habits

Underline key sentences that help you understand the meaning of the word "aircrew."

How can you use clues in the sentences to figure out what a word means?

Think

I'll reread paragraph 2 to see what kinds of clues I can find.

1 Circle the word "controls" in the article, and write the word in the top box of the chart. Then write clues that help you understand what the word "controls" means. Write what you think the word means.

Word:	
First Clue	
Second Clue	
Meaning	

Talk

2 Work with a partner to figure out the meaning of the word "baggage" in the article.

 **Write**

3 **Short Response** What are two clues from the article that help you know the meaning of "attendants"? Write your answer in the space on page 166.

HINT Look for the word "attendants" to find how it is used and what it means.

An Amazing Rescue

by Rebekah Cohen

1   On August 5, 2010, a mine in the country of Chile caved in. Thirty-three men were trapped inside. They were deep below the earth's surface. Finding a way to rescue the workers took a long time. The men were trapped for 69 days.

2   The men say that working together saved them. They voted on all the important decisions. They also took turns doing different tasks. On one day, a miner might be in charge of looking for a way out. On another day, he might keep the underground area clean. They also worked together to make their food last as long as they could.

3   Many people asked how the men stayed so cheerful during their time underground. They took turns keeping each other's spirits up. If they hadn't worked together, the men might have lost hope. But the 33 miners from Chile supported each other to the end. On October 13, 2010, they were saved at last!

Close Reader Habits

What made this rescue "amazing"? **Underline** the clues from the passage that tell why it is amazing.

Think

1 Read this sentence from the article.

They were deep below the earth's surface.

What is the meaning of "earth's surface" in this sentence?

A body of water

B highest point

C deep tunnel

D outside part

> If I don't know a word, I look for clues in the words around it. This helps me figure out what the word means.

2 In paragraph 2, what is the meaning of the word "tasks"?

A rest

B jobs

C turns

D days

Talk

3 Talk with a partner about how the men "supported" each other. Use clues from the passage in your discussion.

Write

4 **Short Response** In paragraph 3, the author says that "the 33 miners from Chile supported each other to the end." Write a sentence from the article that gives a clue about the meaning of the word "supported." Now tell what the word "supported" means. Write your answer in the space on page 167.

> **HINT** Review the passage to find the text clues for the word "supported."

Write Use the space below to write your answer to the question on page 163.

Taking Flight on a **Jumbo Jet**

3 **Short Response** What are two clues from the article that help you know the meaning of "attendants"?

> **HINT** Look for the word "attendants" to find how it is used and what it means.

_____

_____

_____

_____

_____

_____

> Don't forget to check your writing.

Write Use the space below to write your answer to the question on page 165.

An Amazing Rescue

4 **Short Response** In paragraph 3, the author says that "the 33 miners from Chile supported each other to the end." Write a sentence from the article that gives a clue about the meaning of the word "supported." Now tell what the word "supported" means.

> **HINT** Review the passage to find the text clues for the word "supported."

_____

_____

_____

_____

_____

_____

Check Your Writing

☐ Did you read the question carefully?

☐ Can you say the question in your own words?

☐ Did you use proof from the text in your answer?

☐ Are your ideas in a good, clear order?

☐ Did you answer in full sentences?

☐ Did you check your spelling, capital letters, and periods?

▶ **Read**

WORDS TO KNOW

As you read, look inside, around, and beyond these words to figure out what they mean.

- **temperature**
- **heartbeat**
- **operation**
- **medicine**

Who Works in a Hospital?

by Tiffany Gibson

1   A hospital is a busy place! It may even seem confusing at first. Many patients, the people who need to see a doctor, come in every day. Visitors come to see their sick family member or friend. Doctors, nurses, and other hospital workers move calmly from job to job. They know just what to do. They want to give sick or hurt patients the care they need.

2   The hospital medical staff is made up of teams of doctors and nurses. Doctors must examine patients to find the best way to make them better. They check each patient's temperature and heartbeat. They also ask lots of questions. Then doctors think up plans to make each patient better. Some patients will need special medicine. Other patients may need to have an operation. A person who is sick or hurt must stay in the hospital for a few days.

3   Nurses take care of patients who are in the hospital. Some nurses help doctors with operations or special tests. They make sure patients improve each day. They check that the patients are getting better with the right medicine.

4   There are other workers who help the hospital run smoothly. Some workers give X-rays to find out if someone has a broken bone. Others carry out tests to find out why a patient is sick. Some workers make healthy meals or keep hospital rooms clean.

5   Hospital workers do many different jobs, but they all work together. And they work hard! Their goal is to give all patients the care they need to get better.

Think Using what you learned by reading "Who Works in a Hospital?," respond to the following questions.

1 What is the meaning of the word "patients"? Write what "patients" means based on the clues in the sentence.

> **Many patients, the people who need to see a doctor, come in every day.**

_____

_____

2 What is the meaning of the phrase "medical staff" in paragraph 2?

    A   people who keep files of plans

    B   people who treat the sick

    C   people who keep things clean

    D   people who prepare meals

3 Read these sentences from paragraph 2 of the passage.

> **Doctors must examine patients to find the best way to make them better. They check each patient's temperature and heartbeat. They also ask lots of questions.**

What does the word "examine" mean?

    A   make plans for

    B   do surgery on

    C   give medicine to

    D   check over carefully

4 The following question has two parts. First, answer Part A. Then answer Part B.

Part A
Use the chart to write the clues for the phrase "hospital workers." Write the phrase in the first box. After you write the clues, write what you think the phrase means.

Phrase:	
Clue	
Meaning	

Part B
What is the goal of all the hospital workers?

    A   check that the patients are getting better

    B   give the patients the care they need to get better

    C   check each patient's temperature and heartbeat

    D   keep files about the doctors' plans

5 In paragraph 3, the author says, "They make sure patients improve each day." What does the word "improve" mean? Write a sentence from the passage that gives a clue about the meaning of the word "improve."

_____

_____

Write what you think the word "improve" means.

_____

_____

 Write Why is a hospital a busy place?

6 **Plan Your Response** The title of the passage is "Who Works in a Hospital?" It begins with the sentence "A hospital is a busy place!" Find clues in the passage that tell why it is a busy place.

Busy Place

Clue One	Clue Two	Clue Three

7 **Write an Extended Response** Write about the information you found to tell why a hospital is a busy place.

_____

_____

_____

_____

_____

_____

_____

_____

_____

_____

Learning Target

Now that you know how to figure out the meanings of important words in a text, how does this help you better understand the topic?

_____

_____

_____

_____

 **Introduction**

LAFS.2.RI.2.5 Know and use various text features (e.g., captions, bold print, subheadings . . .) to locate key facts or information in a text efficiently.

Lesson 11
Text Features, Part 1 (Captions, Bold Print, Subheadings)

 **Learning Target**

Using text features to find information in nonfiction text will help you better understand what you read.

▶ **Read** Stores use signs and pictures to help you find what you need. Writers use special signs called **text features** to help you find important ideas and details in a text. **Captions, bold print,** and **subheadings** are types of text features to look for when you read.

Read the passage below about igloos. What text features do you see?

House of Snow

An **igloo** is a house made of snow. Some people in snowy areas still make igloos today.

Making an Igloo

Igloos are built with large blocks of packed snow. The snow is cut with a saw or knife. The blocks are then stacked tightly together in the shape of a dome.

The window in this igloo is made of sea ice.

▶ **Think** Look again at the article about igloos. Then fill in the chart below to tell about three text features.

Text Feature	Purpose
caption	
bold print	
subheading	

▶ **Talk** Using the information in your chart, talk to your partner about how text features help you find information as you read.

◎ **Academic Talk**
Use these words and phrases to talk about the text.
- **text features**
- **subheadings**
- **bold print**
- **captions**

Sod Houses

by Henry Wallace

1   Have you ever heard of a **sod** house? Sod is a layer of dirt. It has grass growing on it. Long ago, pioneers used sod to build houses all across the American prairie.

Why People Built Sod Houses

2   The **prairie** looked like a sea of grass. There were not many trees that pioneers could use to build houses. So they cut bricks out of sod instead.

A family and their sod house in Nebraska

Building a Sod House

3   Making sod bricks was not easy. The roots from prairie grasses were tough. They were hard to cut through. Pioneers stacked up sod bricks while the roots were still growing. After a while, the bricks would grow together to make a strong wall.

4   Sod houses kept pioneers cool in the summer and warm in the winter. They also protected them from storms.

Close Reader Habits

Circle text features that help you find information in the article.

Explore   How do the text features in "Sod Houses" help you find information?

> I'll look at all the text features in the article and think about what they tell me.

▶ **Think**

1. Fill in the answers in the chart to tell about the text features in the passage.

Text Feature	Purpose	Examples from Article
bold print		
	tells about the topic of the text that comes after it	
		A family and their sod house in Nebraska

▶ **Talk**

2. Which text feature helped you the most as you read the article on sod houses?

 Write

3. **Short Response** Which text features helped you find out what sod is and how to build a house from it? Write your answer in the space on page 180.

> **HINT** Use the details from your chart to help you answer the question.

▶ **Read**

Homes Around the World

by Coriander Singh

1   People have all kinds of **homes,** or places where they live. Some families live in houses. Other families live in apartments in large buildings. People around the world live in homes like these. They also live in homes you may never have heard about.

A Home People Can Take Apart

2   Some people live in huts. **Huts** are small, simple homes. They are made from branches that are covered with cloth. These homes are easy to put up and take apart. If it's time to move, people can take their homes with them.

Eight people can live on this houseboat.

A Home That Floats on Water

3   Some people live on houseboats. **Houseboats** are homes that float on water and can travel on rivers and lakes. Some houseboats have many rooms, just like houses do on land.

How All Homes Are Alike

4   No matter where they are, all homes are the same in some ways. They protect us from the rain and the sun. They give us a safe place to live, work, sleep, and eat.

Close Reader Habits

How do text features help you find information in a passage? **Put a box** around each subheading. **Circle** the words in bold print, and **underline** their meanings.

▶ **Think**

1 Why is the word **"Huts"** in bold print?

   A   to help you know what huts look like

   B   to show that it is an important word in the passage

   C   to tell about the topic of the text that comes after it

   D   to help you find information about apartments

> Rereading the subheadings will remind me what is in the article.

2 Which text feature helps you find information about homes that can travel on rivers?

   A   the bold print word **"homes"**

   B   the bold print word **"Huts"**

   C   the subheading "A Home People Can Take Apart"

   D   the subheading "A Home That Floats on Water"

▶ **Talk**

3 How can the text features in the article help you understand the information you read about houseboats?

 ▶ **Write**

4 **Short Response** How do subheadings help make the facts in this article easier to find? Write your answer in the space on page 181.

> **HINT** Reread the subheadings. What kinds of details would you find under each one?

Write **Use the space below to write your answer to the question on page 177.**

Sod Houses

3 **Short Response** Which text features helped you find out what sod is and how to build a house from it?

> **HINT** Use the details from your chart to help you answer the question.

_____

_____

_____

_____

_____

_____

_____

Don't forget to check your writing.

Write **Use the space below to write your answer to the question on page 179.**

Homes Around the World

> **HINT** Reread the subheadings. What kinds of details would you find under each one?

4 **Short Response** How do subheadings help make the facts in this article easier to find?

_____

_____

_____

_____

_____

_____

Check Your Writing

☐ Did you read the question carefully?

☐ Can you say the question in your own words?

☐ Did you use proof from the text in your answer?

☐ Are your ideas in a good, clear order?

☐ Did you answer in full sentences?

☐ Did you check your spelling, capital letters, and periods?

▶ **Read**

Abe Lincoln's Cabin

WORDS TO KNOW
As you read, look inside, around, and beyond these words to figure out what they mean.

- **chores**
- **ax**
- **chalkboard**

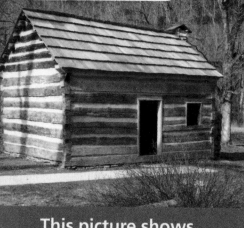

This picture shows what Abe Lincoln's first log cabin looked like. Lincoln was born in Kentucky in 1809.

from *Scholastic News*

1   Long ago, Abraham Lincoln was President of the United States. He was born in a small, one-room log cabin. His family built it themselves. Let's go inside and see what it was like.

Water Bucket and Ax

2   Young Abe had many chores to do. He had to get water for his family because they needed water for washing, drinking, and watering plants. Abe used a bucket to get water from a stream.

3   Abe had another job. He chopped wood with an ax, and his family used the wood for fences and firewood.

Abe's cabin

This picture shows a spinning wheel from Lincoln's time.

Spinning Wheel

4   In Abe's time, people made their own clothes. Abe's mother used a spinning wheel. She put cotton on the wheel and turned the wheel. The cotton stretched out and became thread. She used the thread to make clothes for the whole family.

Slate and Books

5   Abe learned how to read and write in the cabin. He wrote on a small chalkboard called a slate, and he wrote with chalk.

6   Abe loved to read. He would walk miles to borrow books. When he carried his books back to the cabin, he tied them together using leather straps. One of his favorite books was about George Washington.

Games

7   Have you ever heard of jacks? Some people play jacks today, and children also played it in Abe's time. They played a game called cup and ball too. They would try to swing the ball into the cup.

Think Use what you learned by reading "Abe Lincoln's Cabin" to respond to the following questions.

1 This question has two parts. First, answer Part A. Then answer Part B.

Part A
Which information can you find under the subheading "Spinning Wheel"?

   A   what kind of clothes people wore in Abe's time

   B   how Abe's mother used a spinning wheel to make thread

   C   how many times Abe's mother used a spinning wheel

   D   why people made their own clothes in Abe's time

Part B
Write **two** details from the text that show why you chose your answer in Part A.

- The cotton streched out and made thread.
- She put cotton on the wheel and turned the wheel.

2 What do you learn from the caption under the illustration on page 182?

   A   how a spinning wheel works

   B   how Abe gathered water

   C   when Abe was born

   D   what chores Abe had

3 Which subheading came above information about the chores Abe did?

A "Water Bucket and Ax"

B "Spinning Wheel"

C "Slate and Books"

D "Games"

4 Which facts are found under each subheading in the passage? Write the letter of the fact in the correct box in the chart.

A One favorite game was cup and ball.

B Abe chopped wood for the fire.

C Spinning wheels turned cotton into thread.

D Abe would walk miles to borrow books.

E Abe got water from a stream.

F Abe wrote on a slate with chalk.

G Abe's mom made clothes for the whole family.

Water Bucket and Ax	Spinning Wheel	Slate and Books	Games
Abe chopped wood for fire. Abe got water from the stream	Spinning wheels turned cotton into thread Abe's mom made clothes for the whole family	Abe would walk miles to borrow books Abe wrote on a slate with chalk	One favorite game was cup and ball.

5 Read this sentence from paragraph 1.

> He was born in a small, one-room log cabin.

What does "cabin" mean in this sentence?

A a room on a ship

B a baby's room

C a hospital

(D) a small house

6 Which text feature would help you find facts about how Abe learned to read and write?

(A) the subheading "Slate and Books"

B the subheading "Games"

C the caption "This picture shows a spinning wheel from Lincoln's time."

D the caption "Abe's cabin"

 Write What did Young Abe do?

7 **Plan Your Response** Make a list of chores, games, and other things.

Chores	Games	Other
water bucket, and chopping wood.	Cup and ball Jacks	borrow books wrote on slate.

8 **Short Response** What is something you found out about Young Abe? Choose a chore, game, or other activity. Write what it is and what Abe did.

Young abe had to chop
fire wood to keep his
family warm in the winter.

 Learning Target

How does knowing about text features help you find information in a nonfiction text?

It helps me by telling
me that the info
that I need is somewhere
in the text.

 **Introduction**

LAFS.2.RI.2.5 Know and use various text features (e.g., ... glossaries, indexes ...) to locate key facts or information in a text efficiently.

Lesson 12
Text Features, Part 2 (Glossaries, Indexes, Tables of Contents)

Learning Target

When you know the features in a text, including glossaries, tables of contents, and indexes, you can use them to find information.

▶ **Read** Books have text features you can use to help you find and understand **key facts,** or important ideas. These features include tables of contents, glossaries, and indexes.

- A **table of contents** is at the front of a book. It lists the sections or chapters of the book. It tells what information is in each section.

- A **glossary** is at the back of the book. It gives the meaning of important words in the text.

- An **index** is at the back of the book. It gives a list of all the topics in a book. The topics are listed in ABC order. It also gives page numbers where the topics are found.

Table of Contents

Glossary

aircraft a machine that can fly

basket the part of a hot air balloon that people ride in

envelope the part of a hot air balloon that holds heated air

Index

▶ **Think** Pretend you are reading a book called *How Electric Cars Work*. Draw a line from each item in "What You Want to Find" to the correct text feature in "Text Feature You Would Use."

What You Want to Find	Text Feature You Would Use
1. the meaning of "accelerator"	index
2. the page number where you can find information about the battery	table of contents
3. a list of chapters about electric cars in the book	glossary

▶ **Talk** How can text features help you locate information and understand what you read? Talk with a partner about what you learned.

◎ **Academic Talk**
Use these phrases and words to talk about the text.
- **key facts**   - **glossary**
- **index**   - **table of contents**

Read

Genre: Science Text

Hot Air Balloons
By Rachel Nelson

Table of Contents

Chapter 1

What Are Hot Air Balloons?

A hot air balloon is a type of **aircraft.** It has a part inside the balloon called an **envelope.** The balloon rises when the envelope is filled with hot air from a flame. There is a **basket** below the envelope that people can ride in.

Glossary

aircraft a machine that can fly

basket the part of a hot air balloon that people ride in

envelope the part of a hot air balloon that holds heated air

Close Reader Habits

Look at each of the text features on this page, and think about the kind of information they have.

How can text features help you find and understand information about hot air balloons?

▶ **Think**

> I know the table of contents will tell me the topics in the book. I'll read that first.

1 Look back at the text features in *Hot Air Balloons*. Fill in the chart to tell which text feature you would use to answer the questions in the chart.

What You Want to Find	Text Feature You Would Use
Who made the first hot air balloon?	
What does the word "aircraft" mean in the book *Hot Air Balloons*?	
Why does the balloon rise when it is filled with hot air?	

▶ **Talk**

2 How can a table of contents and a glossary help you understand the information in a book? Talk about your ideas with a partner.

▶ **Write**

> **HINT** Think about what each feature does before you write your answer.

3 **Short Response** How can the table of contents and glossary in *Hot Air Balloons* help you locate and understand the information in the book? Write your answer in the space on page 194.

Bullet Trains
by Tiffany Gibson

Introduction

1   People travel from place to place in many different ways. Some ride the bus. Others drive a car. This book explores another kind of transportation: bullet trains!

2   Bullet trains are the fastest trains in the world. Hop on board and hang on tight! This book shares facts about modern bullet trains. Discover which countries and cities use bullet trains today. Find out how fast a bullet train can go. Learn how the trains are made and how they can move so fast. See how many people ride the train each year. You can even learn what energy source bullet trains use.

Index

Countries with bullet trains
    Brazil, 5
    China, 6–9
    Japan, 3–4, 10–11
    Taiwan, 9
    United Kingdom, 2

Energy source, 12
Number of trains, 7
Running a train, 3–12
Speed, 6, 12

Close Reader Habits

How is the index organized? Think about how this can help you quickly locate information you need.

▶ **Think**

1. Look again at the index. On which page can you find information about the kind of energy bullet trains use?

   A page 5

   B page 7

   C page 10

   D page 12

An index is in ABC order. Words under a main topic are also in ABC order. That will help me find what I need.

2. Which page might tell you which cities in China have bullet trains?

   A page 2

   B page 5

   C page 6

   D page 10

3. Would you be able to find key facts on page 10 about the speed of bullet trains? How can you tell?

   _____

   _____

   _____

▶ **Talk**

4. Where would you look if you wanted to find out how bullet trains are run? Talk with a partner about why you would look there.

 ▶ **Write**

5. **Short Response** What information about bullet trains is included in the passage? How can the index help you find more information about bullet trains in this book? Write your answer in the space on page 195.

HINT Think about what you know about each part of a book before you write your answer.

Write Use the space below to write your answer to the question on page 191.

Hot Air Balloons

3 **Short Response** How can the table of contents and glossary in *Hot Air Balloons* help you locate and understand the information in the book?

> **HINT** Think about what each feature does before you write your answer.

_____

_____

_____

_____

_____

_____

_____

> Don't forget to check your writing.

Write **Use the space below to write your answer to the question on page 193.**

Bullet Trains

5 **Short Response** What information about bullet trains is included in the passage? How can the index help you find more information about bullet trains in this book?

> **HINT** Think about what you know about each part of a book before you write your answer.

_____

_____

_____

_____

_____

_____

_____

Check Your Writing

☐ Did you read the question carefully?

☐ Can you say the question in your own words?

☐ Did you use proof from the text in your answer?

☐ Are your ideas in a good, clear order?

☐ Did you answer in full sentences?

☐ Did you check your spelling, capital letters, and periods?

▶ **Read**

Genre: Magazine Article

Kids on the High Seas

text and photographs by Dave and Jaja Martin, *Click*

WORDS TO KNOW

As you read, look inside, around, and beyond these words to figure out what they mean.

- **voyage**
- **wedge**
- **skim**

1 Chris, Holly, and Teiga live on a sailboat. With their mom and dad, they sail all over the world.

2 One summer they sail from the United States all the way across the ocean to a country called Iceland. The voyage lasts 23 days.

3 That's a long time to spend on a small boat at sea. But everything the children need is on board. They have food, water, clothes, and toys. They don't have a television, but they have fun coloring, reading books, and listening to music.

4 During mealtimes in a storm, Chris, Holly, and Teiga wedge themselves onto a bunk. That's a bed built into a wall. Mom hands them bowls of food and they eat slowly. When they are finished, Mom takes the bowls away and hands them cups of juice. It's too bumpy to hold a bowl and a cup at the same time.

5 The best part of a storm is when it's over. The children have to stay inside the cabin. When the sea is smooth again, they can go on deck and play.

6   At first, the middle of the ocean seems empty. All you see are water and sky. But if you look hard, you'll notice a lot. Even far away from land, birds skim the water searching for food. Dolphins swim under the front of the boat, called the bow. If you are lucky, you might see a huge whale gliding across the water's surface. Sooner or later, you spot land.

7   On the twenty-third day at sea, the children see the hills of Iceland. As the boat sails nearer to land, they begin to see lighthouses, then buses, cars, and people walking!

8   Exploring Iceland will be fun, but Chris, Holly, and Teiga can't wait to set sail again. Exploring the ocean is their family's favorite thing to do.

Glossary

bow the front of a boat

bunk a small bed built into a wall in the sailboat's cabin

cabin a room in the lower inside part of a boat

deck the main, outside floor of a boat

sailboat a boat that uses sails to move along the water

Index

Think Using what you learned by reading "Kids on the High Seas," respond to the following questions.

1 Look at the index. Which entry would **most likely** help you find information about who first sailed across the Atlantic Ocean?

    A Sailors of Long Ago

    B Parts of a Sailboat

    C Safety at Sea

    D Sea Creatures

2 Use this glossary entry to answer the question that follows.

> **wedge** (wej) *noun* **1.** A piece of wood or metal that is thick on one end and thinner on the other end: *He used a wedge to keep the door open. verb* **2.** to push into a small space: *The cat wedged itself under the couch. verb* **3.** to keep something from moving by using a wedge: *The window was wedged open.*

Underline the meaning above that **best** matches how "wedge" is used in the following sentence from the passage.

> During mealtimes in a storm, Chris, Holly, and Teiga <u>wedge</u> themselves onto a bunk.

3 Which entry in the index would **most likely** help you learn more about the information in paragraph 6?

    A Sailors of Long Ago

    B Parts of a Sailboat

    C Safety at Sea

    D Sea Creatures

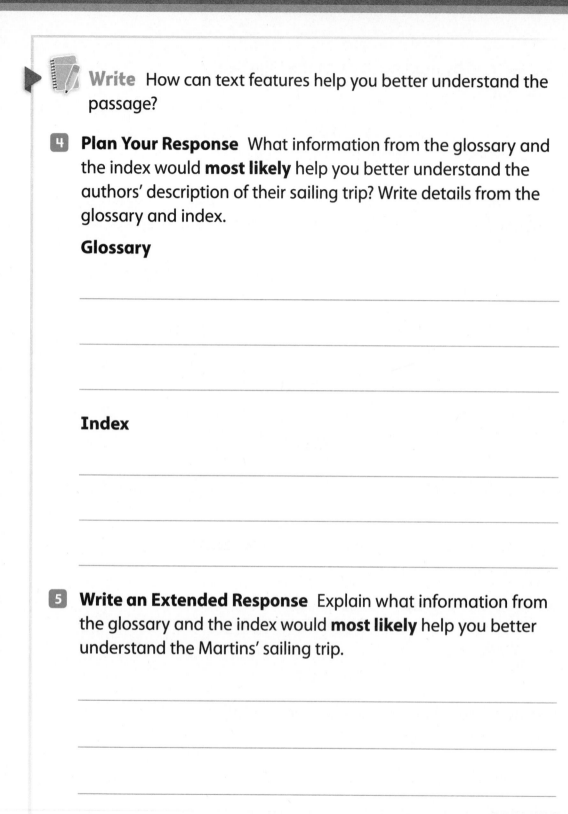

✏️ **Write** How can text features help you better understand the passage?

4 Plan Your Response What information from the glossary and the index would **most likely** help you better understand the authors' description of their sailing trip? Write details from the glossary and index.

Glossary

_____

_____

_____

Index

_____

_____

_____

5 Write an Extended Response Explain what information from the glossary and the index would **most likely** help you better understand the Martins' sailing trip.

_____

_____

_____

_____

_____

_____

Learning Target

How does knowing about text features such as indexes, glossaries, and tables of contents help you quickly find information?

Lesson 13
Author's Purpose

Learning Target

Understanding what an author wants to explain or describe will help you find the main purpose of a text.

▶ **Read** Authors write for different reasons. They write to **describe** what something is like or give **details** to **explain** something. As you read, use details from the text to figure out the author's **main purpose** for writing.

Read the passage below. Think about what the author wants the reader to know.

Three months ago, our garden was just a patch of dirt. Now it's a rainbow of colors! There are smooth, red tomatoes, bright green cucumbers, shiny red and orange peppers, and snowy white cauliflower.

Underline four details that name what's growing in the garden.

▶ **Think** Complete the chart to learn about the author's main purpose for writing this passage.

What is the topic of the passage?	What does the author tell about the topic?	Why did the author write this passage?

▶ **Talk** What is the main purpose of this passage? Talk with your partner about the details that help you understand why the author wrote it.

◎ **Academic Talk**
Use this phrase and words to talk about the text.
- **main purpose**   • **details**   • **explain**   • **describe**

> **Read**

George Crum: Inventor

by Otto Klein

1   You may love crunchy, salty potato chips. But do you know who first made them? A man named George Crum did in 1853. He invented them by accident.

2   Crum was a cook who made delicious French fries. But one day, a man complained. He said the fries were too thick.

3   Crum made the fries thinner, but the fussy man still wasn't happy. So Crum made the fries so thin and crunchy that the man couldn't eat them with his fork.

4   Instead of being angry, the man loved them! Other people who tried Crum's treat also loved them.

5   A few years later, George Crum opened his own restaurant. A big basket of potato chips was placed on every table.

6   In 1895, the first potato chip factory was built. Now people could buy potato chips at the store and put them on their own tables.

Close Reader Habits

Underline two details that tell why Crum made the fries thinner.

Explore   **What is the author's main purpose for writing this passage?**

> Remember, the author's main purpose for writing the text is what the author wants you to know.

▶ **Think**

1   Complete the chart to help you understand the main purpose of the passage.

What is the topic of the passage?	What does the author tell about the topic?	Why did the author write this passage?

▶ **Talk**

2   Why does the author tell about French fries? Talk about it with a partner.

 Write

3   **Short Response**   Why did the author write this passage? Use the information in the chart to explain the author's main purpose. Write your answer in the space on page 208.

> **HINT** Use details from the passage in your answer.

Bananas Are Best

by Julian Green

1   Americans eat many kinds of fruit. Apples and oranges are popular. But when it comes to your health, bananas are one of the best. And here's why.

2   Bananas are made mostly of sugars and fiber. Eating a banana can give you a boost of energy. The fiber helps that energy to last. Bananas are also great sources of vitamins. For example, vitamin C helps you fight a cold. Bananas have more sugars and vitamins than apples or oranges.

3   One important fact is that bananas are high in potassium. Potassium helps your stomach digest food, and it helps your brain stay healthy. Bananas can help keep your eyes and bones strong.

4   It doesn't hurt that bananas taste great! You can slice one up and put it on your cereal. You can bake it into bread or even a pie. Eat a banana every day, and you will be healthier and happier. After all, everyone knows a banana has appeal, and a peel, too!

Close Reader Habits

How do bananas help your stomach and brain? **Underline** the words that tell you.

▶ **Think**

1　This question has two parts. Answer Part A. Then answer Part B.

> This article tells me why bananas are a healthy food. Knowing this helps me figure out the author's main purpose for writing.

Part A
What is the author's main purpose for writing "Bananas Are Best"?

　　A　to tell why bananas are good for you

　　B　to tell what bananas are made of

　　C　to tell how bananas help you fight colds

　　D　to tell what you can do with bananas

Part B
How do details in the article help you figure out the author's main purpose for writing it?

　　A　They explain why bananas have so much sugar.

　　B　They answer questions about bananas.

　　C　They describe what bananas look, taste, and smell like.

　　D　They explain how eating bananas helps your body.

▶ **Talk**

2　What does the author explain in the article?

▶ **Write**

3　**Short Response**　Write about details in the article that help you understand the author's main purpose for writing it. Write your answer in the space on page 209.

> **HINT** What idea is found in every paragraph?

Write Use the space below to write your answer to the question on page 205.

George Crum: Inventor

3 **Short Response** Why did the author write this passage? Use the information in the chart on page 205 to explain the author's main purpose.

> **HINT** Use details from the passage in your answer.

_____

_____

_____

_____

_____

_____

_____

Don't forget to check your writing.

Write Use the space below to write your answer to the question on page 207.

Bananas Are Best

3 **Short Response** Write about details in the article that help you understand the author's main purpose for writing it.

> **HINT** What idea is found in every paragraph?

_____

_____

_____

_____

_____

_____

_____

Check Your Writing

☐ Did you read the question carefully?

☐ Can you say the question in your own words?

☐ Did you use proof from the text in your answer?

☐ Are your ideas in a good, clear order?

☐ Did you answer in full sentences?

☐ Did you check your spelling, capital letters, and periods?

▶ **Read**

Apple Picking Time

from *Weekly Reader*

1   How does the fruit get to our stores?

From the Tree to You

2   Follow an apple from the tree to the store.

3   Fall is apple season! That is when most apples are ripe. Ripe apples are fully grown. They are ready to be picked.

4   Apples grow in orchards. An orchard is a kind of farm. It has rows and rows of apple trees. How does the fruit make its way to you?

5   Workers pick apples. They put the apples into bags. Workers climb ladders to reach apples in tall trees.

6   The apples are put into large bins. Trucks take the bins to a warehouse. That is a building where things are stored. The rooms are kept cold so the apples stay crunchy.

7   The apples are sorted by color and size. Rotten apples are thrown out. The good apples are packed in boxes.

8   Trucks take the apples to grocery stores across the country. The apples are unloaded and placed on shelves.

9   People go to grocery stores to buy apples. They bring them home and eat them. Crunch!

Eating Healthy

Junk food move over! Many schools across the country are getting students to eat healthy foods. University Heights Elementary School in Jonesboro, Arkansas, takes part in a healthy foods program. The students eat all kinds of fruits and vegetables. "I think it's good that we're trying new things," says Justin Livingston, age 7. "I'm crazy about the fruits!"

▶ **Think** Use what you learned from reading "Apple Picking Time" to respond to these questions.

1 Which sentence from the article **best** shows what the author wants to explain?

    A "Ripe apples are fully grown."

    B "The rooms are kept cold so the apples stay crunchy."

    C "How does the fruit make its way to you?"

    D "The students eat all kinds of fruits and vegetables."

2 Number each sentence to tell the correct order of events in the article.

_____ Apples are sorted and packed in boxes.

_____ People shop at the store and take apples home.

_____ Apples are taken to the store and put on shelves.

_____ Workers pick the apples.

_____ Apples are taken to the warehouse.

3 What **best** explains why the author wrote "Apple Picking Time"?

    A to describe how workers pick apples

    B to explain how apples get from trees to stores

    C to answer questions about a school in Arkansas

    D to explain when apples are ready to be picked

4 How do details in the article help you figure out the author's main purpose for writing it?

    A They answer questions about where apples grow and who grows them.

    B They explain the steps taken to get apples from an orchard to a store.

    C They describe different kinds of apples.

    D They describe different kinds of junk food.

5 Tell the author's main purpose for writing the information in the box "Eating Healthy." Then give two details that helped you figure out why the author wrote it.

Author's main purpose for writing "Eating Healthy":

_____

_____

_____

_____

Two details that helped me understand the main purpose:

• _____

_____

• _____

_____

6 Read the sentence from the passage.

> The apples are unloaded and placed on shelves.

To "load" means to move an object into something. What does the word "unloaded" mean in this sentence?

- **A** taken out of
- **B** placed on
- **C** put behind
- **D** pushed away from

Write How do the details in "Apple Picking Time" help you find its main purpose?

7 **Plan Your Response** Write three details from the passage that help you understand its main purpose.

_____

_____

_____

_____

8 **Short Response** Explain the author's main purpose for writing "Apple Picking Time." Use details from the passage in your answer.

_____

_____

_____

_____

_____

Learning Target

How does understanding what the author wants to explain or describe help you find the main purpose of the text?

Read

Read the history article. Then answer the questions that follow.

Flying Dreams

by Emiliana Gutierrez

1   For thousands of years, people have dreamed of flying. That dream finally came true on December 17, 1903. The Wright brothers flew an airplane powered by a motor.

2   Other inventors had tried and failed. They could not control the plane. When it lost its **balance**, the plane would tip, roll, spin, or dive. How did the Wright brothers solve this problem? They watched things closely. They learned lessons from what they saw. Then they put those lessons to work.

Bike Riders and Birds

3   The brothers learned their lessons from bike riders and birds. They saw how riders **bank**, or lean, when they make a turn. When riders turn left, they lean left. When they turn right, they lean right. The brothers saw that pilots must also bank into turns.

4   Birds also bank when they make a turn. They also bend the tips of their wings. The wings of an airplane must bend, too.

Banking and Bending

5   Banking into turns was not a problem. The pilot could lean left or right, just like a bike rider. But how could the pilot bend the tips of the wings? The brothers solved this problem. They made wings of soft cloth on a wooden frame. The pilot pushed a **pedal** connected to **control wires**. The wires pulled on the wings. The wings bent, just like a bird's wings.

6   That first successful powered flight happened on a windy beach in North Carolina. It lasted only 12 seconds and covered only 127 feet. But nothing like it had ever happened before. History had been made!

Glossary

balance: being able to move or keep still without falling

bank: to lean sideways in making a turn

control wires: wires connected to the pedal and to the wings of the plane to bend the wings

pedal: a lever pushed by the pilot's foot to make the wings of the plane bend

This photo shows the first flight of the Wright Flyer. Orville Wright is lying on the lower wing at the controls.

▶ **Think**

1 Read paragraph 2 of the passage.

> **Other inventors had tried and failed. They could not control the plane. When it lost its balance, the plane would tip, roll, spin, or dive. How did the Wright brothers solve this control problem? They watched things closely and learned lessons from what they saw. Then they put those lessons to work.**

What does the word "inventor" mean?

A someone who sells something new

B someone who teaches something

C someone who creates something new

D someone who tells about something

2 Read the sentences from the passage.

> **The pilot pushed a pedal connected to control wires. The wires pulled on the wings.**

What information can you find in the glossary that helps you understand how the pedal on the Wright Flyer worked?

The sides of the Air plane.
To help the Air plane fly.

3 What is the author's main purpose for writing "Flying Dreams"?

A to describe how pilots can make airplanes spin, roll, and dive

B to show what the Wright brothers learned about making airplane motors

C to explain what makes airplanes move like birds in flight

D to tell how the Wright brothers solved problems to help them fly a plane

4 What do you learn from the caption under the photo on page 217?

    A which Wright brother built the plane

    B which Wright brother flew the plane

    C where the Wright brothers' plane is now

    D why the Wright brothers flew their plane

5 Which facts are found under each subheading in the passage?
Write the letter of the fact in the correct box in the chart.

    A The brothers' first flight was just 12 seconds long.

    B The brothers studied how bike riders turn.

    C The brothers decided that pilots should bank to turn.

    D The brothers used a pedal to bend the plane's wings.

    E The brothers used cloth for their plane's wings.

    F The brothers realized that the wings should bend.

Bike Riders and Birds	Banking and Bending

6 Read paragraph 6 from the passage.

    The Wright brothers finally made it work. The first successful powered flight happened on a windy beach in North Carolina. It lasted only 12 seconds and covered only 127 feet. But nothing like it had ever happened before. History had been made!

Underline the sentence that **best** tells what the word "successful" means in this paragraph.

▶ Read

Read the science article. Then answer the questions that follow.

Sue the Dinosaur

by Richard T. Banks

1   Very long ago, a *T. rex* dinosaur died. Sand and mud covered its body. Slowly, the bones turned to rock. They became fossils. The bones stayed covered for a long time. Then wind and water slowly ate away at the earth. Some of the bones poked out of the ground.

Sue is a *T. rex*. The skeleton can be seen at the Field Museum in Chicago.

How Sue Was Found

2   In 1990, fossil hunters were working in South Dakota. One of the women found small pieces of bone on the ground. Then she saw even bigger bones on the cliff above her. When she climbed up the cliff, she saw that the bones were huge!

3   The team all rushed to look. The bones were from a
T. rex! They named the dinosaur Sue after the woman
who had found her.

Why Sue Is Special

4   Other *T. rex* skeletons had been found before. But
Sue's skeleton was one of the biggest and the best.
More than 200 of Sue's bones were found.

5   Scientists worked for years to clean and reconstruct
the skeleton. Finally, they finished putting all the
bones together. Now everyone could see what Sue
had looked like.

**Sue's head is 600 pounds! It's too heavy to put on the skeleton,
so it's inside a glass case in the museum. The head you see on
Sue's skeleton is made of plastic.**

▶ **Think**

7 This question has two parts. First, answer Part A. Then answer Part B.

Part A
What does the word "reconstruct" mean under the subheading "Why Sue Is Special"?

  Ⓐ to clean something old
  B to work hard
  C to find again
  D to put back together

Part B
Underline **one** sentence in the paragraphs below that **best** supports the answer in Part A.

   Other *T. rex* skeletons had been found before. But Sue's skeleton was one of the biggest and the best. More than 200 of Sue's bones were found.

   Scientists worked for years to clean and reconstruct the skeleton. Finally, they finished putting all the bones together. Now everyone could see what Sue had looked like.

8 Choose **three** facts that are found under the subheading "Why Sue Is Special."

  A the number of bones in Sue's skeleton
  Ⓑ how Sue's bones turned into fossils
  C what scientists did with the skeleton
  D where fossil hunters found Sue
  E how Sue the dinosaur got her name
  F how Sue is different than other *T. rex* skeletons

9 Look at the index below from a book about dinosaurs.

> **Index**
> Baby dinosaurs
>   colors,   6
>   eggs,   5
>   nests,   5-7
>   size,   8
> How fossils form,   9
> North America
>   dinosaur fossils,   10-15
>   fossil hunters,   11

Which page would **most likely** tell you more about the person who found Sue?

A page 5

B page 6

C page 8

D page 11

10 This question has two parts. First, answer Part A. Then answer Part B.

Part A
Why did the author write "Sue the Dinosaur"?

A to tell about the famous skeleton of a *T. rex*

B to explain why fossil hunters were in South Dakota

C to tell how the bones of a dinosaur are put together

D to describe how fossils are made and where to find them

Part B
Underline the sentence below that **best** tells about the answer in Part A.

   Other T. rex skeletons had been found before. But Sue's skeleton was one of the biggest and the best. More than 200 of Sue's bones were found.

Write

Extended Response What does the word "fossil" mean in "Sue the Dinosaur"?

11   **Plan Your Response** Reread "Sue the Dinosaur" to help you write about the meaning of the word "fossil."

First, write a sentence from the passage that has the word "fossil" in it.

They Became fossil.

Now write another sentence from the passage that helps you know what "fossil" means.

The bones that stayed covered for a long time.

Write your own sentence with the word "fossil" in it.

The fossil henters were not so nice.

12 **Write an Extended Response** What does the word "fossil" mean in "Sue the Dinosaur"? Use details from the passage in your answer.

_____

_____

_____

_____

_____

_____

_____

_____

_____

_____

_____

_____

_____

_____

Unit 4

Craft and Structure in Literature

If you want to make art, you need to make some choices. Do you want to use paint or pencils? What colors will you use?

Authors also make choices. They choose words that help them tell a story. They also pick words for the sounds they make or the pictures they help you imagine.

In this unit, you will find out how authors choose their words. You'll learn how these words help you understand stories, poems, and songs. You will also learn how to be a great storyteller. And you'll pay special attention to what characters say and do.

✔ Self Check

Before starting this unit, check off the skills you know below. As you complete each lesson, see how many more skills you can check off!

I can:	Before this unit	After this unit
tell how word sounds give meaning to a story.	✓	☐
tell how words give rhythm and meaning to a poem or song.	☐	✓
tell about the beginning, middle, and end of a story.	✓	☐
find the differences in characters' points of view.	☐	☐
show differences in the way characters say their words.	☐	☐

page 230

page 236

page 244

page 250

page 264

page 279

page 289

Lesson 14
Sound and Meaning in Stories

Learning Target

Describing the special ways that authors use words and sounds will help you get more meaning from stories you read.

▶ **Read** Authors use words in special ways. They may use **repetition,** or repeated words and ideas, to show that something is important. Authors also use words that begin with the same letter or sound, like "**g**ray **g**oose." This is called **alliteration.** Repetition and alliteration can add meaning to a story. They can also make the sentences fun to read.

Read the sentences that go with each picture. How did the writers use words and sounds in special ways?

The sky is falling!
The sky is falling!

The silly snail slid down the rail.

▶ **Think** Look again at the pictures and the sentences. Fill in the chart with examples that show special ways the authors used words and sounds. Then tell what the words do to add meaning.

What Is It Called?	Examples	What Do the Words Do?
repetition		They show that something is important.
alliteration		

▶ **Talk** Have you heard or read other examples of repetition or alliteration? Talk about this with a partner. Make a list to share with others.

 Academic Talk
Use these words to talk about the text.
• **repetition** • **alliteration**

Read

Crow Sings a Song

from Aesop

1   One day, Fox strolled by just as Crow was about to eat her breakfast. She held a large piece of cheese in her beak. Fox loved cheese. Fox loved cheese a lot. So he came up with a plan for getting some of it for himself.

2   "Dear Crow!" Fox said in his nicest voice. "You are the most beautiful of birds. Your black feathers are so shiny. Your beak is perfectly pointy!"

3   "I have also heard about your fine singing," he sighed. "I would so love to hear you sing just one song."

4   Crow had never trusted Fox, but she loved to be admired. Her wings began to flutter and flap with pride.

5   Crow pointed her beak up to the sky. She opened her mouth and cawed just a little. Then she opened her mouth again and caw-cawed a bit louder. Finally, she opened her mouth wide and caw-caw-CAWED out a song that was heard across the forest. But, of course, the cheese fell out of her beak!

6   "Ha!" cried Fox, as he caught the tasty treat. "I knew I could trick you, you croaky old Crow."

7   And with that, Fox ran off with his prize. Crow felt ashamed. She had lost her breakfast for being too proud!

Close Reader Habits

Circle examples of alliteration in paragraph 2.
Underline the repeated words in paragraph 5.

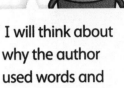

Explore **How does the author use words and sounds in special ways to add meaning to the story?**

> I will think about why the author used words and sounds in the story.

▶ **Think**

1 Look at these sentences from the story. Tell what each is called. Then tell how each one adds meaning.

Examples	What Is It Called?	What Do the Words Do?
"Fox loved cheese. Fox loved cheese a lot."		
"Her wings began to flutter and flap with pride."		

▶ **Talk**

2 Fox speaks in his nicest voice to Crow. Find examples of alliteration that help make his words sound good to Crow.

▶ **Write**

3 **Short Response** How does the repetition in paragraph 5 add meaning to the story? Write your answer in the space on page 234.

> **HINT** What changes every time the crow opens her beak?

Jungle Parade

by Steven Krensky

1   One day, Monkey was feeling bored. Then he got an idea. He swung his arms back and forth, hummed a happy tune, and started marching through the jungle. He marched to the left. He marched to the right. One step, two steps, taking-just-a-few steps.

2   Lion decided to follow him, shaking his mane. Three steps, four steps, listen-to-me-roar steps.

3   Elephant soon joined them, raising his trunk. Five steps, six steps, careful-don't-do-kicks steps.

4   Then Kangaroo came along, and Giraffe and Zebra and Cockatoo got in line behind her. Seven steps, eight steps, keep-the-line-real-straight steps.

5   In the big jungle parade, all the animals were bending and bowing and bumping to the beat. Paws went up and hoofs went down. They stepped and stomped all over the ground.

6   Hours passed, and the sun went down. So the animals marched to the left and they marched to the right. Soft steps, slow steps, off-to-bed-we-go steps.

Close Reader Habits

Underline the sentences at the ends of paragraphs 1, 2, 3, 4, and 6. How are they alike?

Think

1 Look again at paragraph 5.

> In the big jungle parade, all the animals were bending and bowing and bumping to the beat. Paws went up and hoofs went down. They stepped and stomped all over the ground.

> This story had a lot of alliteration and repetition. I'll think about how the words add meaning to the story.

Underline the examples of alliteration that you see.

2 The author repeats a similar sentence at the end of most of the paragraphs. What does the repetition help you understand?

A Giraffe, Zebra, and Cockatoo are the only animals marching in a straight line.

B Although some of the animals have their own way of stepping, they are all part of the same parade.

C Because Monkey starts the parade, he is the best marcher.

D Elephant doesn't march well because he keeps kicking other animals.

Talk

3 Look again at the examples of alliteration you underlined from paragraph 5. How do they add to the fun of the story?

 Write

4 **Short Response** How is the first paragraph like the last one? Why do you think the author did this? Write your answer in the space on page 235.

> **HINT** Which ways do the animals march each time?

Write **Use the space below to write your answer to the question on page 231.**

Crow Sings a Song

3 **Short Response** How does the repetition in paragraph 5 add meaning to the story?

> **HINT** What changes every time the crow opens her beak?

_____

_____

_____

_____

_____

_____

_____

> Don't forget to check your writing.

Write Use the space below to write your answer to the question on page 233.

Jungle Parade

4 **Short Response** How is the first paragraph like the last one? Why do you think the author did this?

> **HINT** Which ways do the animals march each time?

_____

_____

_____

_____

_____

_____

_____

Check Your Writing

☐ Did you read the question carefully?

☐ Can you say the question in your own words?

☐ Did you use proof from the text in your answer?

☐ Are your ideas in a good, clear order?

☐ Did you answer in full sentences?

☐ Did you check your spelling, capital letters, and periods?

▶ **Read**

Picnic Guests

by Cynthia Reeg, *Ladybug*

1   Buddy napped in the noonday sun.

2   His furry golden belly faced the blue sky. His four legs stuck straight up like fuzzy fence posts.

3   Crrrunch! Crrrackle! Crrrunch!

4   Buddy's eyelids popped open. What was that noise?

5   Crrrunch! Crrrackle! Crrrunch! The noise came from somewhere in the grass, and it was growing louder.

6   Suddenly Buddy jumped back. Something was marching toward him.

7   A long parade of something very tiny and very noisy. A parade of ants!

8   Buddy blinked his eyes. The tiny insects carried teeny forks and knives. Some lugged lawn tents and chairs. "Where are you going?" Buddy asked.

9   "To a picnic, of course," said the ant leader. "Why don't you come along with us?"

10   Buddy snorted in surprise. "Why, thank you," he said. "That's very kind of you."

11   Buddy looked carefully at the ants marching through the grass. Something was missing.

12   "Excuse me," said Buddy. "I'd love to join you, but I think you've forgotten something for your picnic."

13   "Forgotten something!" The ant leader stopped. "What could we possibly have forgotten?"

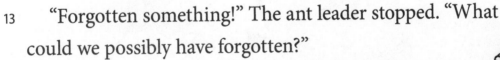

14   "Why, the food, of course," said Buddy.

15   All the ants squealed with laughter. The ant leader pointed to Buddy's food dish.

16   "The food is already there!"

17   Buddy gulped. That was his food! He felt a snarl forming.

18   But then Buddy looked at the giggling ants. His snarl stopped halfway up his throat. These ants were guests. His guests. A slow smile pulled on the corners of his mouth.

19   "Woof! Woof!" barked Buddy. "Welcome!" He grabbed his favorite ball and joined in the picnic parade.

▶ **Think** Use what you learned from reading the selection to respond to these questions.

1 Which of the following is an example of alliteration in the story?

A "furry golden belly"

B "fuzzy fence posts"

C "teeny forks and knives"

D "corners of his mouth"

2 This question has two parts. First, answer Part A. Then answer Part B.

Part A
Reread paragraphs 6 and 7.

> Suddenly Buddy jumped back. Something was marching toward him.
>
> A long parade of something very tiny and very noisy. A parade of ants!

Which words are repeated?

very , very

Part B
Look at the words you wrote in Part A. Which answer below **best** explains why these words are repeated?

A to show that the ants were very small

B to show that the ants look and sound like a parade

C to show that Buddy is slowly figuring out what he's seeing

D to show that Buddy was frightened by the parade of ants

3 Read this sentence from paragraph 11.

> Buddy looked carefully at the ants marching through the grass.

What is the base word for the word "carefully"?

A full

B care

C are

D fully

4 Which answer **best** explains why "guests" is repeated in paragraph 18?

A to show that the ants are not going to stay with Buddy

B to show that Buddy finally understands how to treat the ants

C to show that Buddy does not want to join the picnic parade

D to show that the ants are polite enough to bring their own forks and knives

 Write How do words and sounds add meaning to the story?

5 **Plan Your Response** Look in the selection for examples of alliteration. Make a list of your choices.

6 **Short Response** Choose **two** examples of alliteration in the story. Tell how they add to the meaning.

_____

_____

_____

_____

_____

_____

_____

_____

_____

_____

⊙ Learning Target

Why should you look for examples of alliteration and repetition when you read?

_____

_____

_____

_____

Introduction

LAFS.2.RL.2.4 Describe how words and phrases (e.g., regular beats, . . . rhymes . . .) supply rhythm and meaning in a . . . poem or song.

Lesson 15
Rhythm and Meaning in Poems and Songs

 **Learning Target**

Describing how poets use rhythm and rhyme will help you understand how both can add meaning to a poem.

▶ **Read** Poets choose their words carefully. Sometimes they pick words that create a **regular beat** when you read them out loud. This regular beat, or **rhythm,** is what makes you want to clap your hands or tap your foot.

Poets may also use words that **rhyme.** These words have the same end sound, as in *tin* and *chin*. Rhyme can help connect ideas in words or lines in a song or poem.

Read this song out loud. Clap your hands to the beat. Listen for words that rhyme.

Twinkle, twinkle, little star,
How I wonder what you are!

Up above the world so high,
Like a diamond in the sky.

Twinkle, twinkle, little star,
How I wonder what you are!

▶ **Think**

1 Read the first two lines again. The check marks show which syllables have the strongest beats. Mark the second line in the same way.

      ✓   ✓   ✓   ✓

Twin-kle, twin-kle, lit-tle star,

How I won-der what you are!

2 Look at the two lines again. Which words rhyme? Circle them.

Twinkle, twinkle, little star,

How I wonder what you are!

▶ **Talk** Look at what you marked in number 1. What do you notice about the words or syllables with check marks? Look at what you circled in number 2. Where do you find the rhyming words? Talk with a partner about the rhythm of the song.

> ◎ **Academic Talk**
> Use these words and phrase to talk about the text.
> • **rhythm**   • **regular beat**   • **rhyme**

There Was an Old Donkey Named Joe

by Andrea Sanders

There was an old donkey named Joe,

Whose best friend was Alice the Crow.

They made a fine pair,

Alice danced on Joe's hair,

And they each wore a bright-colored bow.

Close Reader Habits

Circle one set of words that rhyme. **Draw boxes** around another set. Think about where each set of words is in the poem.

Explore   How do rhyme and rhythm make this poem fun to read?

▶ **Think**

> I'll read the poem out loud and listen to the rhythm and rhyme.

1 Read the poem aloud. Finish putting check marks over the strongest beats.

> ✓   ✓   ✓
> **There was an old donkey named Joe,**
>
> **Whose best friend was Alice the Crow.**
> ✓   ✓
> **They made a fine pair,**
>
> **Alice danced on Joe's hair,**
>
> **And they each wore a bright-colored bow.**

2 Write two sets of rhyming words from the poem.

Set 1 _Crow and Joe_

Set 2 _Pair hair_

▶ **Talk**

3 How do the rhymes help connect lines in the poem? Tap out the rhythm and talk about how it changes in each line.

 ▶ **Write**

4 **Short Response** Look again at the marks you made in question 1. Which two lines have a different rhythm? What do those two lines describe? Write your answer in the space on page 248.

> **HINT** What do lines 3 and 4 tell you about Alice and Joe?

Read

My Lizard

by Elizabeth Tidy, *Highlights*

A lizard sat upon my wall.

He looked so happy, green, and small.

"What scaly thoughts are in your head?"

"I'm thinking of my bike," he said.

5 "Your bike?" with shock I did reply.

"I did not know that you could ride

A bicycle. I thought you crawled

Across the ground and right up walls."

"Yes, well, you are mistaken, lad,"

10 My lizard said, a wee bit mad.

And from behind my potted plant,

He took a bicycle and sat

Upon its teeny tiny seat

And peddled off with lizard feet.

Close Reader Habits

Circle two pairs of words that rhyme in the first four lines of the poem.

Think

1 Find four sets of rhyming words in the poem. Write them in the chart.

Rhyming words have the same end sound, but the sound may not be spelled the same way.

Set 1	Set 2	Set 3	Set 4

Talk

2 Read the poem aloud. Clap on the strong beats. Mark the strong beats in each line. How would you describe where the strong beats fall? How does the rhyme make you feel when you read the poem?

HINT Think about how the rhythm and rhyme make you feel about what the speaker sees.

 ## Write

3 **Short Response** Is the poem silly or sad? How do the rhythm and rhyme help? Write your answer in the space on page 249.

Write Use the space below to write your answer to the question on page 245.

There Was an Old Donkey Named Joe

4 **Short Response** Look again at the marks you made in question 1. Which two lines have a different rhythm? What do those two lines describe?

> **HINT** What do lines 3 and 4 tell you about Alice and Joe?

_____

_____

_____

_____

_____

_____

Don't forget to check your writing.

Write Use the space below to write your answer to the question on page 247.

My Lizard

3 **Short Response** Is the poem silly or sad? How do the rhythm and rhyme help?

_____

_____

_____

_____

_____

_____

_____

Check Your Writing

☐ Did you read the question carefully?

☐ Can you say the question in your own words?

☐ Did you use proof from the text in your answer?

☐ Are your ideas in a good, clear order?

☐ Did you answer in full sentences?

☐ Did you check your spelling, capital letters, and periods?

▶ **Read**

I Love the World

by Eileen Spinelli, *Highlights*

WORDS TO KNOW

As you read, look inside, around, and beyond these words to figure out what they mean.

- **sweeping**
- **view**
- **scarlet**
- **vine**

I love the world when it is white,
when snowflakes fall in winter light
to cover everything in sight.

I love the world when it is blue—
5   a sweeping, rented beach-house view:
blue sea, blue sky, blue dolphins, too.

I love the world when it is green,

with fields of corn and climbing bean

and rows of peppers in between.

10   I love the world when it is red,

when scarlet leaves make mice a bed

and sunset crimsons overhead.

Each season's grace and gifts are mine—

the purple hills, the silver vine . . .

15   And so, dear world, this valentine.

▶ **Think** Use what you learned from reading "I Love the World" to respond to these questions.

1 This question has two parts. First, answer Part A. Then answer Part B.

Part A
Which is the **best** description of what this poem looks like?

    A   The poem has 15 lines.

    B   The poem has five sets of three lines.

    C   The poem is divided into two main parts.

    D   The poem begins each group of lines the same way.

Part B
Which sentence explains how rhyme is connected to your answer in Part A?

    A   Rhyme is used at the beginning and end of the poem.

    B   Rhyme connects important pairs of words.

    C   The three lines in each set end with words that rhyme.

    D   Only one part of the poem has words that rhyme.

2 Reread lines 1, 4, 7, and 10. What happens on the last strong beat of each one?

    A   The sentence ends.

    B   A season is named.

    C   A plant is listed.

    D   A color is named.

3 Mark the strong beats in each line with a check mark. Then describe the rhythm.

I love the world when it is white,

when snowflakes fall in winter light

_____

_____

_____

4 Reread lines 10–13. Which **two** words are made up of smaller words that help you figure out their meaning?

A scarlet, sunset

B crimsons, scarlet

C sunset, overhead

D overhead, scarlet

Write what you think each of these words means.

_____

_____

_____

5   Which sentence tells how the last set of three lines in the poem is different from the other sets?

     A   The three lines don't rhyme.

     B   The first line does not begin the same way as the others.

     C   It mentions a holiday instead of a time of year.

     D   The rhythm is different.

6   Why does the poet begin lines 1, 4, 7, and 10 with the words "I love"?

_____

_____

▶ **Write**   Which part of the poem is your favorite?

7   **Plan Your Response**   Reread the poem to choose the part that you like best. Remember to look for things such as rhyme and rhythm.

8   **Short Response**   Use details from the poem to tell which part of the poem is your favorite. Talk about rhythm or rhyme if you can.

_____

_____

_____

_____

_____

_____

_____

Learning Target

How do rhythm and rhyme add meaning to any poem you read?

_____

_____

_____

Lesson 16
Parts of a Story

Learning Target

Knowing how the beginning, middle, and end of a story work together will help you understand what you read.

▶ **Read** All stories have a beginning, middle, and end. The **beginning** introduces, or first tells about, the characters and the **problem** they face. The **middle** shows how the problem gets bigger. The **end** tells how the problem is **solved,** or worked out.

Look at the cartoon below. What is happening in each part of the story?

Beginning

Middle

End

What problem does the boy have?
How does his dad help him solve it?

▶ **Think**   Using what you see in the cartoon, think about what happened to the boy. Then complete the chart by describing what happens in each part.

Beginning	
Middle	
End	

▶ **Talk**   Think about what you see in the cartoon. What will the boy do next?

> ◎ **Academic Talk**
> Use these words to talk about the text.
> - **beginning**   - **problem**   - **solved**
> - **end**   - **middle**

Jasper
the Farm Cat

by Henry Adamson

1   Jasper was a farm cat. His job was to catch mice in the barn. The people he lived with didn't want mice in the barn. The mice ate the horses' grain. As you know, most cats like catching mice. But Jasper wasn't like most other cats. He had become friends with the mice in the barn. He didn't want to catch them.

2   "What am I going to do?" said Jasper to Millie, one of his mouse friends. "If I don't catch you, my people might want to get rid of me. And I like it here!"

3   For days, Jasper worried about what to do. Then he had an idea. He was always seeing the people he lived with throw away food scraps in the kitchen. All this food just went to waste. If he snuck these food scraps to the mice, then they wouldn't have to eat the horses' grain!

4   So that's just what he did. And everyone was happy. Jasper's people saw that the mice were no longer taking the horses' grain. The mice had food to eat. And Jasper had his friends.

Close Reader Habits

Underline sentences that tell about Jasper's problem.

Explore How do the beginning, middle, and end of "Jasper the Farm Cat" work together?

> I'll figure out what the problem is and how it's solved.

▶ **Think**

1 Fill in the chart with details from the story.

Beginning	• Who is Jasper? • What is Jasper's problem? He had to work so hard to get the mice out the barn
Middle	
End	

▶ **Talk**

2 Take turns with your partner describing what happened in the beginning, middle, and end of the story.

 **Write**

3 **Short Response** Think about how the story ends. Why is Jasper's idea a good one? Use details from the story in your answer. Write your answer in the space on page 262.

> **HINT** How does everyone feel at the end of the story?

The Case of the Missing Mutt

by John Hansen

1   Mrs. Brown stood at the gate in her backyard with a puzzled look on her face. As I walked closer, I could see something was wrong. Mrs. Brown wiped tears from her eyes and said, "I think someone has stolen Snippets!"

2   Snippets was Mrs. Brown's dog. I asked her why she thought he had been stolen. She said the gates were all closed tight, so he couldn't have just run off.

3   I took a look around. Some leaf bags stood piled near one corner. I told her Snippets could have easily hopped up on the bags and over the fence.

4   "But Marty," she said, "why would he do that?"

5   "Most likely to see another dog," I said. I asked her if Snippets had ever been to the new dog park. Mrs. Brown said, "Why, yes! My granddaughter took him there last week."

6   I found Snippets playing with his friends at the park. I promised I would take him back there later. But first there was someone who very much needed to see him.

Close Reader Habits

What problem does Marty need to solve? **Underline** clues that help you figure it out.

Think

1 What is Mrs. Brown's problem at the beginning of the story?

   A Mrs. Brown thinks someone has stolen her dog, Snippets.

   B Marty doesn't want to help Mrs. Brown.

   C Snippets has become lost in the dog park.

   D Snippets has found a way to open the gate.

> I'm going to look for details about the characters and the problem at the start of the story.

2 When does Marty first get the idea that Snippets wasn't stolen?

   A when he finds Mrs. Brown crying

   B when he sees the leaf bags by the fence

   C after Mrs. Brown talks about her granddaughter

   D after he goes to the dog park

Talk

3 Talk with a partner about why Mrs. Brown thinks Snippets was stolen. Be sure to use details from the story.

Write

4 **Short Response** How is Mrs. Brown's problem solved? Use details from the story in your answer. Write your answer in the space on page 263.

> **HINT** What does Marty ask Mrs. Brown?

Write Use the space below to write your answer to the question on page 259.

Jasper the Farm Cat

3 **Short Response** Think about how the story ends. Why is Jasper's idea a good one? Use details from the story in your answer.

> **HINT** How does everyone feel at the end of the story?

_____

_____

_____

_____

_____

_____

_____

> Don't forget to check your writing.

Write **Use the space below to write your answer to the question on page 261.**

The Case of the Missing Mutt

4 **Short Response** How is Mrs. Brown's problem solved?
Use details from the story in your answer.

> **HINT** What does Marty ask Mrs. Brown?

_____

_____

_____

_____

_____

_____

Check Your Writing

- ☐ Did you read the question carefully?
- ☐ Can you say the question in your own words?
- ☐ Did you use proof from the text in your answer?
- ☐ Are your ideas in a good, clear order?
- ☐ Did you answer in full sentences?
- ☐ Did you check your spelling, capital letters, and periods?

▶ **Read**

THE Shade SELLER

A Korean Folktale

by Marilyn Helmer, *Spider*

1   A magnificent shade tree once grew near the house of a greedy merchant. Every day, the merchant sat under the tree.

2   One warm day a young man stopped to rest under the tree, too.

3   "Ho!" cried the merchant. "What do you think you're doing, sitting in my shade?"

4   "The tree belongs to everyone," he said.

5   "It is mine. However, I am willing to sell you the shade," declared the merchant.

6   "No one owns shade," said the young man.

7   "I own the tree, therefore I own the shade," replied the merchant. The young man paid the greedy merchant.

8   As the hours passed, the shade moved with the sun.

9   When the shade moved into the merchant's yard, the young man did, too. The merchant frowned.

10   Then the shade moved onto the merchant's front porch. The young man followed. The merchant gritted his teeth.

11   Finally, the shade moved right into the merchant's magnificent house. The young man moved right in with it. This was more than the merchant could tolerate.

12   "What do you think you are doing?" he shouted.

13   "I'm simply following my shade," said the young man. The young man had, indeed, bought the shade.

14   The next day the young man returned and brought his relatives. His children laughed and played in the shade. His uncles and cousins sang and danced.

15   The merchant could hardly hear himself think. Finally, he shouted, "I want to buy back my shade."

16   "You sold it to me, and I intend to keep it," the young man shouted back. The merchant retreated to his house in frustration.

17   Soon after that, the merchant moved far away. The young man moved into the magnificent house. And to this day travelers are welcome to share the shade.

Think Use what you learned from reading "The Shade Seller" to answer the following questions.

1 What do we learn about the merchant at the beginning of the story?

    A He often argues with people who sit in his yard.

    B He doesn't like it when people sing and dance.

    Ⓒ He sits under the tree near his house every day.

    D He doesn't know that shade moves with the sun.

2 This question has two parts. First, answer Part A. Then answer Part B.

Part A
When does the problem begin?

    Ⓐ when the merchant finds the young man sitting where the merchant likes to sit

    B when the young man says that no one owns shade

    C when the merchant yells at the young man for moving into his house

    D when the young man brings his relatives to the merchant's house

Part B
Write the sentence that tells what the merchant wants the young man to do in order to sit in the shade of the tree.

He wanted him to pay in order to sit in the shade.

3 At the beginning of the story, the author says that the merchant is greedy. Find two details in the story that show the merchant is greedy. Write them on the lines below.

"What do you think your doing, sitting in my shade. "I am willing to sell you the shade.

4 The young man brings his family to the house. Read the sentence that tells what the merchant did.

The merchant retreated to his house in frustration.

What does "retreated to" mean in this context?

    A went away from

    B went back inside

    C looked behind

    D tore down

Theo

▶ **Write** How does the merchant's problem change during the story?

5 **Plan Your Response** Below are details from "The Shade Seller."
Write them in the part of the chart where they **best** fit.

The family moves into the house for good.
The young man follows the shade into the house.
The merchant sells his shade to the young man.
The young man brings his family to enjoy the shade.
A young man stops to rest under a tree.
The merchant moves away.

Beginning	A young man stops to rest under a tree. The merchant sells the shade to the young man
Middle	The young man follows the shade into the house. He bring his family to share the shade
End	The merchant goes away The family moves into the house for good.

6 **Write an Extended Response** How did the merchant's problem change during the story? Explain what happened and whether the problem was ever solved. Use details from the story in your answer.

The problem wasn't solved because the merchant moved away and the family kept the shade and the house for good.

©Curriculum Associates, LLC   Copying is not permitted.

Theo

 Learning Target

Explain how the parts of a story work together. How do the three parts make the story interesting?

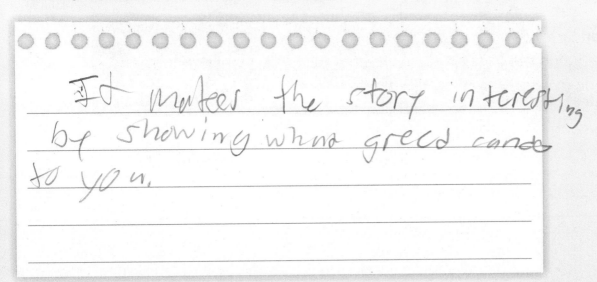

It makes the story interesting by showing whna greed cando to you.

 **Introduction**

LAFS.2.RL.2.6 Acknowledge differences in the points of view of characters, including by speaking in a different voice for each character when reading dialogue aloud.

Lesson 17
Point of View

 **Learning Target**

Knowing that characters in a story can have different points of view will help you understand how they think and feel about what happens.

▶ **Read** Each **character,** or person in a story, has a point of view. A **point of view** is how a character thinks or feels about other story characters or events.

You can often figure out a character's point of view by looking closely at the **dialogue,** or what is said. You can also get clues from how the character acts. When you read a story out loud, you can change your voice to show different characters' points of view.

Look at the picture below. What is each character's point of view about the pet lizard?

▶ **Think** Look again at the cartoon. Finish the chart to show each character's point of view. Also write details that helped you figure out the point of view.

Character	Point of View	Details
Girl holding lizard	likes the lizard	has lizard in hands is smiling
Girl with hat		leans toward the lizard
Girl in chair		

▶ **Talk** Read the cartoon aloud. Change your voice to show the characters' different points of view.

⊚ **Academic Talk**
Use these words and phrase to talk about the text.
- **point of view**   - **dialogue**   - **character**

Stage Fright

by Wendy Blake

Setting: Amy's house, after school. Amy and her friend Pete are talking about the play their class is putting on the next day.

1 **AMY:** Can you believe that tomorrow afternoon we'll be on stage in front of the entire school? It's going to be so much fun!

2 **PETE:** I wish there would be a snowstorm tonight. Then maybe we wouldn't have school tomorrow. Too bad it's spring and not winter.

3 **AMY:** Oh, Pete! There's nothing to worry about. We've been practicing for weeks.

4 **PETE:** But what if I forget my lines? I don't think I can do this.

5 **AMY:** You won't forget your lines, silly. We just went through them ten minutes ago, and you were great.

6 **PETE:** (*frowning*) But it's different when you're on stage and everyone is staring at you.

7 **AMY:** Just think about the fun part of acting! You know, the part where you get to pretend you're someone else.

8 **PETE:** (*looks down and shakes his head*) I wish I really were someone else so I wouldn't have to do this tomorrow.

> ### Close Reader Habits
>
> **Underline** sentences in the dialogue that tell you how each character feels about being in the play.

Explore **How are Amy's and Pete's points of view different?**

Theo

▶ **Think**

> I'm going to reread the lines I underlined to help me figure out each character's point of view.

1 Finish the chart to show each character's point of view. Put two or three details in the last column.

Character	Point of View	Details
Amy		
Pete		

▶ **Talk**

2 Take turns reading the play out loud with your partner. How does your voice change to show each character's point of view? Show what you mean.

 Write

3 **Short Response** Why does Pete feel the way he does about the play? Use details from the text in your answer. Write your answer in the space on page 276.

> **HINT** Look for details in the text that show how Pete is feeling.

> **Read**

Skip and Fliss

by Lila Bailey

1   Skip and Fliss were two happy dolphins. They spent their days playing in the ocean.

2   One day, Fliss spotted a bright orange ring floating on the water. She was curious! Fliss slipped her nose through the ring and jumped up in the air.

3   "Hey, look at me!" Fliss shouted to Skip. "I've got a nose ring!"

4   "Mom wouldn't like that," Skip warned. "It could be dangerous."

5   But Fliss was having too much fun. "Don't worry so much, Skip!" she laughed.

6   Skip shook his nose and said, "I'd rather be careful than get into trouble."

7   The next day, Skip and Fliss were playing when Fliss saw something waving in the water. Of course, she swam right over to it. But the pretty waving thing was a fishing net! When Fliss swam too close to it, she got her head caught in the ropes. "Help! Help!" she cried out.

8   Skip quickly swam to her and started pulling hard on the net. Finally, with one big pull, Fliss wriggled free of the net.

9   "Never again will I put my nose where it doesn't belong!" Fliss cried.

10   Fliss still had fun in the sea, but now she stayed away from strange stuff!

Close Reader Habits

What is each character's point of view? **Underline** details that help you figure that out.

Think

1 This question has two parts. Answer Part A. Then answer Part B.

Part A

What is Fliss's point of view at the beginning of the story?

A She likes to have fun and not worry too much.

B She likes to have fun, but she is careful, too.

C She would rather be safe than explore new things.

D She worries about what her mother thinks.

Sometimes a character's point of view can change. See if that happens in this story.

Part B

Which line from the story **best** supports your answer in Part A?

A "Skip and Fliss were two happy dolphins."

B "'Don't worry so much, Skip!' she laughed."

C "'Never again will I put my nose where it doesn't belong!' Fliss cried."

D "Fliss still had fun in the sea, but now she stayed away from strange stuff!"

Talk

2 What is Skip's point of view about exploring strange things? How do you know?

 ## Write

3 **Short Response** How does Fliss's point of view change from the beginning to the end of the story? Why does it change? Use details from the story in your answer. Write your answer in the space on page 277.

HINT What happens to Fliss when she goes over to the net?

Write Use the space below to write your answer to the question on page 273.

Stage Fright

3 **Short Response** Why does Pete feel the way he does about the play? Use details from the text in your answer.

> **HINT** Look for details in the text that show how Pete is feeling.

_____

_____

_____

_____

_____

_____

Don't forget to check your writing.

Write **Use the space below to write your answer to the question on page 275.**

Skip and Fliss

3 **Short Response** How does Fliss's point of view change from the beginning to the end of the story? Why does it change? Use details from the story in your answer.

> **HINT** What happens to Fliss when she goes over to the net?

_____

_____

_____

_____

_____

_____

Check Your Writing

☐ Did you read the question carefully?

☐ Can you say the question in your own words?

☐ Did you use proof from the text in your answer?

☐ Are your ideas in a good, clear order?

☐ Did you answer in full sentences?

☐ Did you check your spelling, capital letters, and periods?

WORDS TO KNOW

As you read, look inside, around, and beyond these words to figure out what they mean.

- **harvest**
- **settled**
- **jingling**
- **flicked**

The Squirrel and the Crow

An Indian folktale retold by Reena I. Perl, *Highlights*

1   Once upon a time a crow and a squirrel owned a field. They agreed to work the field together. One day the squirrel called out to the crow. "Come, Brother Crow. It's time to plow the field." The crow was lazy. He stretched his left wing and his left leg, then said:

"Sister dear, do go ahead.

I will follow soon.

I'll eat this piece of buttered bread

And be with you by noon."

2   The squirrel plowed the field all day. Meanwhile, the crow enjoyed the cool breeze that blew through the tree.

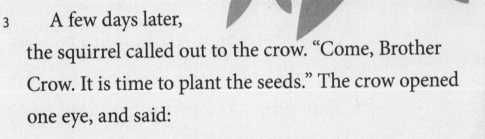

3 A few days later,
the squirrel called out to the crow. "Come, Brother
Crow. It is time to plant the seeds." The crow opened
one eye, and said:

"Sister dear, do go ahead.

 I will follow soon.

I'll eat this piece of buttered bread

 And be with you by noon."

4 The little squirrel planted seeds all by herself. Rain
fell, and before long all the seeds had sprouted. Soon,
every stalk had fat ears of wheat. "Come, Brother
Crow," called the squirrel. "It's time to harvest the
grain." But the crow settled himself in his nest.

5 The squirrel cut down the wheat. Soon there
were piles of golden grain waiting to
be put into sacks.

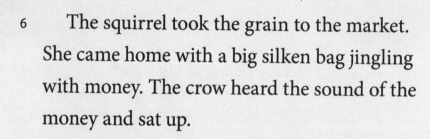

6   The squirrel took the grain to the market. She came home with a big silken bag jingling with money. The crow heard the sound of the money and sat up.

7   "Come, Sister Squirrel," he called greedily. "Let us count and divide the money so I can take my share."

8   The little squirrel dropped the bag into her nest and turned to the crow. Smiling her sweetest smile, she said:

"Brother Crow, there is no share

For lazy birds like you.

When all your buttered bread is gone,

You'll wish you had worked, too."

9   The squirrel flicked her tail and vanished into her nest. The crow sat on his branch feeling very silly.

Think Use what you learned from reading the selection to respond to these questions.

1 Which sentence **best** describes the squirrel's point of view about working in the fields?

    A She prefers to do the work herself.

    B She enjoys plowing and planting.

    C It is hard work, but it has to be done.

    D The work has to be done at a certain time.

2 What is the crow's point of view about hard work?

    A Let others do the work, but all must share the results.

    B Be sure you're well rested before you work.

    C Share the work and share the results.

    D A good friend is always happy to do the work for you.

3 This question has two parts. First, answer Part A. Then answer Part B.

Part A
Underline the sentence that tells the squirrel's feelings about what the crow deserves.

> "Brother Crow, there is no share
> For lazy birds like you.
> When all your buttered bread is gone,
> You'll wish you had worked, too."

Part B
Tell what the sentence you marked in Part A means.

It means that if you are lazy you can't get your share of something.

4 Read these lines from the story.

> "Come, Sister Squirrel," he called greedily. "Let us count and divide the money so I can take my share."

Underline the dictionary definition in the box below that **best** matches this use of the word "share."

---

share *verb*

   1   to have or use something with others (to share toys)

   2   to talk about with others (to share feelings)

share *noun*

   1   a part of something that has been divided equally (a share of the prizes)

   2   the amount you are responsible for (your share of the work)

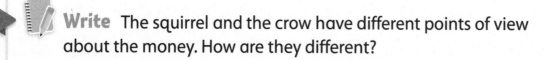 **Write** The squirrel and the crow have different points of view about the money. How are they different?

5 **Plan Your Response** Underline sentences that tell the squirrel's or the crow's point of view about the money.

6 **Short Response** How is the squirrel's point of view about the money she brings home different from the crow's point of view? Use details from the story in your answer.

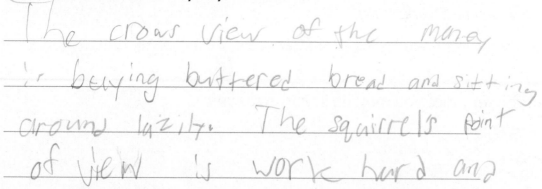

The crows view of the money is buying buttered bread and sitting around lazily. The squirrel's point of view is work hard and

get the money to feed herself
and her young.

Learning Target

**Why is thinking about a character's point of view important
when you tell a story to others?**

It is important to others
because you and others can
see what the characters
point of view is

Read the poem. Then answer the questions that follow.

Boots and the Troll

by Len Larsen

Old Boots had a farm in a land dark and cold.

He chopped wood for his fire and wood to be sold.

But that winter the forest held something quite scary.

A monster called a troll, who was big and mean and hairy!

5   One day Boots was chopping a snow-covered tree,

When he heard the troll growl, "These woods are for me!"

The troll lifted a log and snapped it in two.

He shouted, "Run away now, or this log might be you!"

Next day Boots was chopping another big tree,

10   When he heard the troll growl, "These woods are for me!"

But Boots had a plan, so he just stood his ground.

He took out a cheese that was stone-like and round.

When Boots squeezed the cheese hard, it dripped gooey green goo.

He yelled, "Run away now, or this rock might be you!"

15   The troll heard these words and saw the strange stone.

He turned and ran fast, right back to his home!

Think

1 What is Boots's problem at the beginning of the poem?

    A A troll shows Boots that he can lift a log and snap it in two.

    B A troll doesn't want Boots to chop wood in the forest.

    C Boots doesn't have enough wood to sell.

    D Boots lives on a farm in a dark, cold land.

2 Read lines 3 and 4 of the poem.

> **But that winter the forest hold something quite scary,**
> **A monster called a troll, who was big and mean and hairy!**

Write the two rhyming words in these lines. What do these words help you understand about the poem?

Rhyming words:

What the words help me understand about the poem:

_____

_____

3 The poem has a regular beat. Read the line below and mark each strong beat with a checkmark (✔) above the word.

> **He chopped wood for his fire and wood to be sold.**

How many strong beats are in the line?

    A 1

    B 2

    C 3

    D 4

4 This question has two parts. First, answer Part A. Then answer Part B.

Part A
Read these lines from the poem.

> **When Boots squeezed the cheese, it dripped gooey green goo.**
> **He yelled, "Run away now, or this rock might be you!"**
> **The troll heard these words and saw the strange stone.**
> **He turned and ran fast, right back to his home!**

Which kind of speaking voice would you use to show how Boots feels about the troll?

A a soft voice

B a sad voice

C a loud voice

D a friendly voice

Part B
Why would you use the speaking voice you chose in Part A? Use details from the poem in your answer.

_____

_____

_____

_____

5 What is the troll's point of view about Boots at the end of the poem?

A He thinks Boots is funny.

B He thinks Boots is scary.

C He thinks Boots is messy.

D He think Boots is lucky.

Read the story. Then answer the questions that follow.

Kate Skates

by Rhonda Leverett, *Highlights*

1   Last year, when Carlene moved next door, we started the Carlene and Kate Club. We paint noodle necklaces and make paper masks and eat peanut-butter sandwiches with lots of grape jelly. Sometimes we wear purple and jump around yelling "Purple Power!"

2   Purple makes us ready for anything.

3   But when I saw Carlene's party invitation, I said, "No way!"

Please come to my birthday skate party!

Saturday, 3p.m.

Monroe Ice Rink

4   Carlene loves skating. She takes lessons every Thursday while I'm at ballet. I tried it once, and I spent more time sitting on the ice than skating on it.

5   This morning I hid behind my bed. "I don't want to go to that party."

6   I almost forgot our club's number one rule: we always stick together.

7   "This is really rotten," I said in the car.

8   "You'll be fine," Mom said.

9   I stared out the window.

10   When we got to the rink, I walked toward the party very slowly. I was thinking of reasons to turn around and ask Mom to drive me home. But there were lots of balloons, and the cake was a giant flower, and Carlene gave me a hug. We ate snacks and made funny faces.

11   I'd just started having a great time when someone yelled, "Let's skate!" My heart went *PA-BOOM-BOOM-BOOM*. My knees started shaking.

12   I put on ice skates as *slooowly* as I could. Then I placed one foot on that slippery ice, then the other.

13   "Come on, Kate!" Carlene took my hands and started skating backward. I held on tight. Fast kids whizzed by. Some fell down, too. I held on tighter.

14   "Think about your favorite thing," Carlene said.

15   I remembered my dance recital. The cheering crowd, the butterfly costume, and the spinning, spinning . . . Carlene and I went down—splat!

16   My face felt hot, the way it does when people see me mess up.

17   Then Carlene said, "Hey, we're both wearing purple."

18   It was true—she had a purple hair ribbon, and I had a purple bracelet.

19   I pushed myself up. Slowly.

20   "OK. Let's try again," I said.

21   Even though my knees were shaking, we made it once around the rink. I kind of liked it! Maybe I just needed a little practice.

22   When Carlene opened her present from me, she smiled. It was a bracelet just like the one I was wearing. After she put it on, we held up our matching bracelets. "Purple Power!" we yelled together.

▶ Think

6 Read these sentences from the story.

> **I'd just started having a great time when someone yelled, "Let's skate!"**
> **My heart went *PA-BOOM-BOOM-BOOM*. My knees started shaking.**

What does the repetition of the word "*BOOM*" help the reader understand about Kate?

- **A** Kate is having fun.
- **B** Kate is feeling scared.
- **C** Kate's knees are starting to hurt.
- **D** Kate's heart is beating slowly.

7 Read paragraph 22 below.

> **When Carlene opened her present from me, she smiled. It was**
> **a bracelet just like the one I was wearing. After she put it on, we held**
> **up our matching bracelets. "Purple Power!" we yelled together.**

Underline the example of alliteration in this paragraph.

8 Read the paragraphs from the story.

> **This morning I hid behind my bed. "I don't want to go to that party."**
>
> **I almost forgot our club's number one rule: we always stick together.**
>
> **"This is really rotten," I said in the car.**

What is the **best** meaning of "rotten" as it is used in the story?

- **A** sick
- **B** mean
- **C** terrible
- **D** moldy

9 Below are some events from "Kate Skates." Write these events in the part of the chart where the sentences **best** fit.

Kate goes to Carlene's party.

Kate skates once around the rink with Carlene.

Kate gives Carlene a purple bracelet.

Kate and Carlene fall on the ice.

Kate gets invited to Carlene's party.

Beginning	
Middle	
End	

Write

Extended Response How does Carlene help to change Kate's point of view about skating?

10 **Plan Your Response** Write details from the story that show Kate's point of view about skating for most of the story. Then write details from the story that show what Carlene does to help change Kate's point of view about skating, and how Kate feels about skating at the end of the story.

Kate's point of view about skating for most of the story:

_____

_____

_____

_____

Things that Carlene does that help to change Kate's point of view about skating:

_____

_____

_____

_____

_____

_____

Kate's point of view about skating at the end of the story:

_____

_____

_____

11 **Write an Extended Response** Tell how Carlene helps to change Kate's point of view about skating. Use details from the story in your answer.

_____

_____

_____

_____

_____

_____

_____

_____

_____

_____

_____

_____

_____

_____

_____

_____

_____

_____

_____

Integration of Knowledge and Ideas in Informational Text

What if someone from another planet asked you about cats? You might say, "Cats are furry animals with four legs and a long tail." But would that be enough to show what a cat looks like? You would probably show a picture of some cats, too. Imagine your new friend then asked, "Why do people like cats?" You would give a list of reasons. You might say, "Cats are good friends to people. They are cuddly."

In this unit, you'll see how pictures can show you more about what you read. You'll also learn how authors give reasons for their ideas. You will see how texts about the same topic can be alike and different.

✔ Self Check

Before starting this unit, check off the skills you know below. As you complete each lesson, see how many more skills you can check off!

I can:	Before this unit	After this unit
use pictures in a text to help me understand the passage.	☐	☐
find the important points an author makes in a passage.	☐	☐
find the reasons the author uses to make those points.	☐	☐
compare and contrast the most important points in two texts on the same topic.	☐	☐

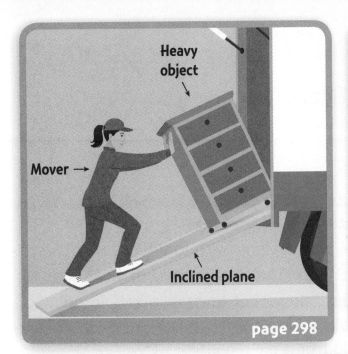

Heavy object

Mover →

Inclined plane

page 298

page 300

page 314

page 319

page 324

page 335

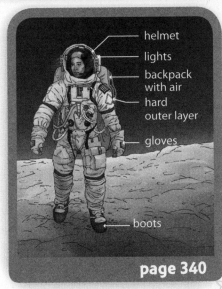

helmet
lights
backpack with air
hard outer layer
gloves
boots

page 340

Lesson 18
Explaining How Images Support Text

 **Learning Target**   **Looking at the pictures that go with a text will help you better understand what you read.**

▶ **Read** When you read, pictures and other **images** can be as important as words. They can **support,** or help explain, information in the text. For example, **diagrams** are drawings that show the different parts of something. They can also show how something works.

Read the sentences. Then look at the diagram. How do they work together to help you understand the parts of a fire truck?

The driver of a fire truck sits in the cab. A ladder and a hose are connected to the main part of the truck. The hose is long and can stretch far from the truck.

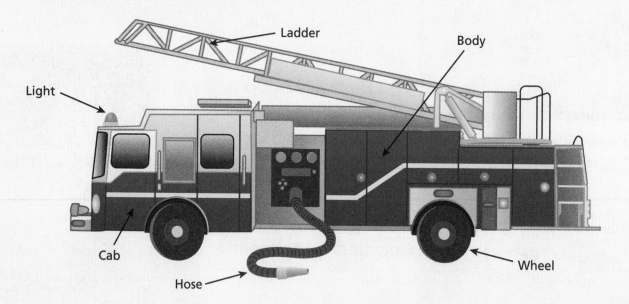

©Curriculum Associates, LLC   Copying is not permitted.

▶ **Think** Look again at the page about the fire truck. Fill in the chart to tell what you learn from the sentences and the diagram.

What the Text Tells	What the Diagram Shows

▶ **Talk** The sentences and the diagram of the truck help you understand the parts of the fire truck. Talk with a partner about how the diagram makes the sentences easier to understand.

Academic Talk
Use these words to talk about the text.

- **support**
- **diagrams**
- **images**

▶ **Read**

The Inclined Plane

by Sandra Brody

1   Many years ago, people had a problem. How could they easily move heavy objects without lifting them? The answer to the problem was the inclined plane.

2   An inclined plane is a flat surface that creates a ramp. This ramp makes a smooth climb from a lower place to a higher place. Inclined planes let people move heavy objects more easily. They can push the objects instead of lifting them.

3   Today, we use inclined planes all the time. Wheelchair ramps are one example. Loading ramps for moving trucks are another. Boat ramps are another.

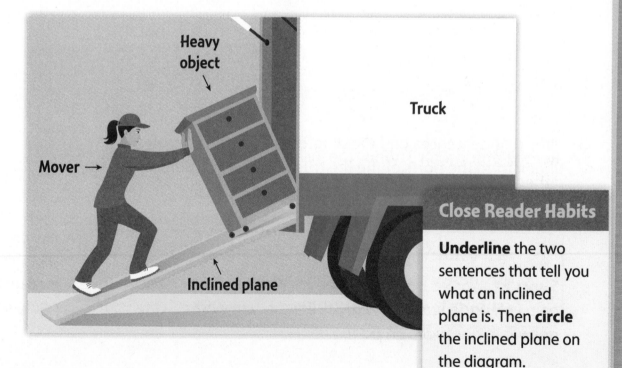

Close Reader Habits

Underline the two sentences that tell you what an inclined plane is. Then **circle** the inclined plane on the diagram.

©Curriculum Associates, LLC   Copying is not permitted.

Explore How does the diagram of an inclined plane help you better understand the information in the article?

> As I reread the text, I will look at the diagram to help me understand.

▶ **Think**

1 Read the article again. Fill in the chart to show how the text and the diagram work together.

What the Text Tells	What the Diagram Shows

▶ **Talk**

2 Reread paragraph 3. What are inclined planes used for? What other reasons can you think of for using an inclined plane?

> **HINT** How does the diagram show what you read about in paragraph 2?

▶ **Write**

3 **Short Response** Look again at the diagram. How does it help you understand how an inclined plane works? Write your answer in the space on page 302.

Wheels and Axles by Ed Green

Wheel

Axle

Wheel

1   A simple machine has few or no moving parts. One kind of simple machine is a wheel and axle. A wheel and axle can help move people or objects from one place to another.

2   Wheels and axles are all around you. Cars and bicycles have wheels and axles. A skateboard has them. Even a Ferris wheel is really just a big wheel and axle!

3   This simple machine has a large wheel. It also has a rod, called an axle. The axle goes through the center of the wheel. When the axle is turned, the wheel also turns.

Close Reader Habits

How does a wheel and axle work? **Put a box around** the paragraph that tells how it works. **Circle** labels on the diagram that show the two parts of this machine.

Think

1 Which sentence from the passage does the diagram help to explain?

> A "A wheel and axle can help move people or objects from one place to another."
>
> B "Wheels and axles are all around you."
>
> C "Cars and bicycles have wheels and axles."
>
> D "The axle goes through the center of the wheel."

After I reread the text, I'll look at the diagram. It will tell me more about what I've read.

2 How does the diagram add to what the author tells us?

> A It shows that the machine can have two or more axles.
>
> B It shows that the axle must be long and heavy.
>
> C It shows that wheels and axles turn in the same direction.
>
> D It shows that many things around us have wheels and axles.

Talk

3 The article says that wheels and axles can help move people or objects from place to place. What does this mean?

HINT Look at the article for examples of things that use wheels and axles.

 ## Write

4 **Short Response** How does this article help you understand how wheels and axles work? Use one detail from the diagram and one detail from the text to support your answer. Write your answer in the space on page 303.

Write Use the space below to write your answer to the question on page 299.

The Inclined Plane

3 **Short Response** Look again at the diagram. How does it help you understand how an inclined plane works?

> **HINT** How does the diagram show what you read about in paragraph 2?

> Don't forget to check your writing.

Write Use the space below to write your answer to the question on page 301.

Wheels and Axles

4 **Short Response** How does this article help you understand how wheels and axles work? Use one detail from the diagram and one detail from the text to support your answer.

_____

_____

_____

_____

_____

_____

_____

Check Your Writing

☐ Did you read the question carefully?

☐ Can you say the question in your own words?

☐ Did you use proof from the text in your answer?

☐ Are your ideas in a good, clear order?

☐ Did you answer in full sentences?

☐ Did you check your spelling, capital letters, and periods?

> **Read**

Genre: Science Article

Levers and Pulleys
by Julian Green

1   What is a machine? You might think it's something that has a motor. But a machine is any tool that helps us move things. Two simple machines are levers and pulleys.

2   A lever is made of a solid bar and a fulcrum. The fulcrum is the spot that the bar rests on. It is close to the object you are lifting. When one end of the bar goes down, the other end goes up, like a seesaw. If one end of the bar is longer than the other, it can be used to lift an object. The object is called the load. With a long, strong lever, you can lift really heavy loads.

Seesaw

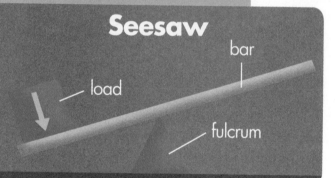

load
bar
fulcrum

Using a Lever

bar

load

fulcrum

3   A pulley is another kind of machine. It can also be used to lift a load. It is made of a rope and a wheel. The rope passes over the wheel. When you pull down on one end of the rope, the other goes up. If something is tied to the rope, it goes up, too. You might have window blinds that work this way.

4   Machines like these have been used for thousands of years. Many of today's biggest machines are still based on levers and pulleys.

wheel

rope

rope

load

Using a Pulley

▶ **Think** Use what you learned from reading "Levers and Pulleys" to respond to these questions.

1 This question has two parts. Answer Part A. Then answer Part B.

Part A
Which of the following **best** tells what a "machine" is?

    A anything that has a motor

    B a tool that helps us move things

    C tools made with wheels and fulcrums

    D anything used to lift heavy loads

Part B
Write the words that name two simple machines.

    motor   lever   fulcrum   pulley   load   pivot

    lever

    pulley

2 Look at the the diagram of the seesaw on page 304. What does the bar rest on?

    A a wheel

    B the load

    C the fulcrum

    D the ground

3 What do the diagrams of a lever and a pulley in the article show?

(A) how to make objects easier to move

B how to have fun with a simple machine

C how to use a rope to lift something

D how to use a bar to move something

4 Look carefully at the diagram showing a person moving a rock. What does it show about using a lever to lift something?

A The center of the bar should rest on the fulcrum.

B The bar should be long and very heavy.

C The fulcrum should be closer to the person.

(D) The fulcrum should be closer to the load.

5 How do the text and the diagrams help you understand the meaning of "load"?

It helps by telling me that load means something that you are putting on a lever or pully.

6 How does the diagram of the pulley help you understand how to use a pulley?

A It shows how to attach the object to the rope.

(B) It shows how pulling down on the rope lifts the object.

C It shows how fast the wheel has to turn.

D It shows how hard a person needs to pull.

7 Write the parts below under "pulley" or "lever." One part will be used twice.

• rope   • bar   • load   • wheel   • fulcrum

pulley	lever
rope load wheel	bar fulcrum load

▶ 📝 **Write** How are levers and pulleys used to move things?

8 **Plan Your Response** Look again at the article. Think about the steps you would follow to use each tool. Make a list of the steps.

9 **Write an Extended Response** Explain how levers and pulleys are used to move things. Use your list and information from both the article and the diagrams in your answer.

Levers and pulley's are used to move things by either a person pulling a load and spinning a wheel without causing friction and by putting a load on a

lever and putting the bar
on a fulcram to lift
the load.

Learning Target

How does looking at the pictures that go with a text help you better understand what you read?

It helps me better understand
by helping me know how the
pully or lever works.

Lesson 19
Describing How Authors Use Reasons to Support Their Ideas

 **Learning Target**

Telling about the reasons authors use to explain the points they make helps you better understand ideas in texts.

▶ **Read** A **key point** is an important idea about a topic. Authors **support** their key points with **reasons.** In a book about insects, an author might say that some insects are good at hiding. The author would support this key point with reasons that explain more about it.

Look at the photos and captions below. How do they support the key point that some insects are good at hiding?

Leaf katydids look like green leaves to blend in with trees and plants.

Walking sticks look like twigs to hide from animals that might eat them.

▶ **Think** Look again at the photos and captions. Write two reasons that support the key point in the chart.

Key Point: Some insects are good at hiding.

Reason:

Reason:

▶ **Talk** Look again at each reason in your chart. Talk with a partner about the way the reasons support the key point.

⊙ **Academic Talk**
Use these words and phrase to talk about the text.
- **key point**
- **reasons**
- **support**

Earwigs

by Jane Kinzer

1   Many people do not like earwigs. These small brown insects scurry up walls, and they have big pincers. But earwigs aren't as bad as you might think.

2   Believe it or not, earwigs make very good mothers. Many insects lay their eggs and then leave. Not earwigs! The mother stays with her eggs, cleaning them and keeping them safe. She even helps the babies hatch out of their eggs. Once they have hatched, she helps them eat. She also keeps them out of danger.

3   Earwigs are also not as scary as they look. Sure, they have wings and big pincers. But they do not use their wings often. And earwigs don't like to use their pincers on humans. They use them mostly to catch prey. Even when they do pinch people, they are just keeping themselves safe. The pincers don't cause any harm.

4   The next time you see an earwig, remember: it's more than just a creepy bug!

> **Close Reader Habits**
>
> **Draw a star** by the sentence that tells the key point of the article. When you reread, **underline** reasons that support the key point.

Explore How does the author show that earwigs are not as bad as they might seem?

▶ **Think**

> I need to look for reasons that explain the key point.

1. Read the key point. Then write the reasons the author uses to support the key point.

Key Point: Earwigs are not as bad as they seem.

Reason:

Reason:

▶ **Talk**

2. After reading the article, do you agree that earwigs are not as bad as they seem? Talk with a partner and tell why.

 **Write**

3. **Short Response** Why don't people have to worry about the earwig's pincers? Use reasons from the text in your answer. Write your answer in the space on page 316.

> **HINT** Reread paragraph 3. What reasons can you use?

Soldier Bees

by Melissa Maron

1   We could learn a lot about working together from honeybees. There are three types of bees in a hive. They all do different jobs to help make their hive a home. The queen bee lays eggs. Drones are the fathers. And worker bees do everything else. They clean the hive, feed the young, and find nectar. In South America, some honeybees have added a new kind of worker: the soldier bee.

2   Soldier bees stay at the opening of the hive to protect it from robber bees. Robber bees like to steal the honey from other hives. In most hives, the worker bees stand guard for only one or two days. Then they fly off to do other jobs. But soldier bees are different. They spend their whole lives defending the hive from other insects. They are very good at keeping the other bees safe. The soldier bees are some of nature's tiny heroes.

Close Reader Habits

What is the key point in paragraph 1 and paragraph 2? **Underline** the key point in each paragraph.

Think

1 What key point does the author make about honeybees in paragraph 1?

I'm going to look for details that support the key point I underlined.

    A   All the bees work to make their hive a home.

    B   The three types of bees are queen, drone, and worker.

    C   Robber bees like to steal honey from other bees.

    D   Soldier bees are a special kind of worker bee.

2 What reason does the author give to explain the key point she makes about honeybees in paragraph 1?

    A   Robber bees like to steal honey from hives.

    B   Each type of bee in a hive does a different job.

    C   Some bees have added a new kind of worker.

    D   Soldier bees are different from worker bees.

Talk

3 The author makes the key point that soldier bees are different from worker bees. What are two reasons from the passage that support this point?

Write

4 **Short Response** Write about how soldier bees are different from worker bees. Write your answer in the space on page 317.

HINT Use reasons that you just talked about in your answer.

Write Use the space below to write your answer to the question on page 313.

Earwigs

HINT Reread paragraph 3. What reasons can you use?

3 **Short Response** Why don't people have to worry about the earwig's pincers? Use reasons from the text in your answer.

_____

_____

_____

_____

_____

_____

_____

Don't forget to check your writing.

Write **Use the space below to write your answer to the question on page 315.**

Soldier Bees

> **HINT** Use reasons that you just talked about in your answer.

4 **Short Response** Write about how soldier bees are different from worker bees.

_____

_____

_____

_____

_____

_____

_____

Check Your Writing

☐ Did you read the question carefully?

☐ Can you say the question in your own words?

☐ Did you use proof from the text in your answer?

☐ Are your ideas in a good, clear order?

☐ Did you answer in full sentences?

☐ Did you check your spelling, capital letters, and periods?

▶ **Read**

Genre: Science Article

Bugs!
Nature's Time Machine

by Nicole Linden

WORDS TO KNOW

As you read, look inside, around, and beyond these words to figure out what they mean.

- **millions**
- **prehistoric**
- **wingspans**

1   Have you ever wondered what insects looked like millions of years ago? They probably looked nothing like insects do today, right?

2   Not so fast. Insects long ago looked a lot like insects today. One kind of bug, the cockroach, has hardly changed at all. It still has a flat body and legs built for running. It still eats many different things, both living and dead. Cockroaches are built in a way that works well for them. In fact, cockroaches might stay the way they are for many more millions of years.

3   Other insects have changed a lot in some ways, and not so much in others. Prehistoric dragonflies looked much like they do today. They had long, thin bodies and two sets of wide wings.

Cockroaches have changed very little over time.

4   But there was one big difference: dragonflies a long time ago were much larger. They had wingspans of up to two feet long. This means that a dragonfly could be as big as a dog! That could cause problems for people today. We are lucky that today's insects are mostly smaller than they once were.

5   Scientists think that many insects have not changed much because they haven't needed to. They were still able to find food and shelter as the world changed. So they didn't need to change themselves.

6   The next time you see an insect squirming in a garden, don't say "Eww!" Instead, look at it closely. You might just be looking into the far-off past!

Long ago, dragonflies had wingspans about as long as your arm!

▶ **Think** Use what you learned from reading "Bugs: Nature's Time Machine" to respond to these questions.

1 This question has two parts. First, answer Part A. Then answer Part B.

Part A
What key point does the author make about cockroaches?

   A Cockroaches have hardly changed at all.

   B Cockroaches have flat bodies and legs that are good for running.

   C Cockroaches eat many different things.

   D Cockroaches used to be much larger.

Part B
What are **two** reasons the writer gives to support the point you chose in Part A?

• _____

_____

_____

• _____

_____

_____

2 The author says that insects today look a lot like they did millions of years ago. Underline three facts to support this key point.

A   Dragonflies from long ago could be as big as a dog.

B   Today's cockroach still has a flat body.

C   Prehistoric dragonflies had long, thin bodies.

D   Cockroaches are built for running.

E   Ancient dragonflies had wingspans of up to two feet.

F   Most insects today are much smaller than they once were.

3 Reread paragraph 5. What key point does this sentence from paragraph 5 support?

They were still able to find food and shelter as the world changed.

A   Insects haven't changed much because they haven't needed to.

B   Some insects have changed a lot in some ways and not so much in other ways.

C   Insects long ago looked a lot like insects today.

D   Cockroaches are built in a way that works well for them.

4 Use the dictionary entry to answer the question.

> **shelter** (shel´ter) *n.* **1.** something that protects from weather or danger *v.* **2.** to shield or hide *n.* **3.** a refuge *n.* **4.** a place for poor or homeless to stay for a while

Which meaning matches how "shelter" is used in this sentence?

They were still able to find food and shelter as the world changed.

A   meaning 1

B   meaning 2

C   meaning 3

D   meaning 4

5 What sentence **best** describes the key point of the entire article?

A   Cockroaches and dragonflies have survived for millions of years.

B   Insects haven't changed much since prehistoric times.

C   Insects are built in ways that allow them to survive.

D   Insects today are smaller and weaker than they once were.

▶ **Write**   Why does the author think it's a good idea to look at insects closely?

6 **Plan Your Response**   Reread the text and underline details that tell you what insects were like millions of years ago and today.

7 **Short Response**   Explain the reasons the author gives to support her point that it's a good idea to look at insects closely. Use details from the text in your answer.

_____

_____

_____

_____

_____

_____

_____

_____

_____

_____

_____

Learning Target

How does understanding the way authors use reasons to support key points help you understand ideas in a text?

Lesson 20
Comparing and Contrasting Two Texts

 **Learning Target**

Comparing and contrasting the most important points in two texts on the same topic will help you learn more about the topic.

▶ **Read** When you **compare** texts, you tell how they are alike. When you **contrast** texts, you tell how they are different. Comparing and contrasting the most **important points** in two texts on the same topic helps you learn more about the topic.

Look at these two posters. How are they alike? How are they different?

Poster 1

Take care of planet Earth. Plant a tree!

Poster 2

Take care of planet Earth. The animals will thank you!

▶ **Think** Look again at the posters. Use the *Venn diagram* below to compare and contrast the important points in each poster.

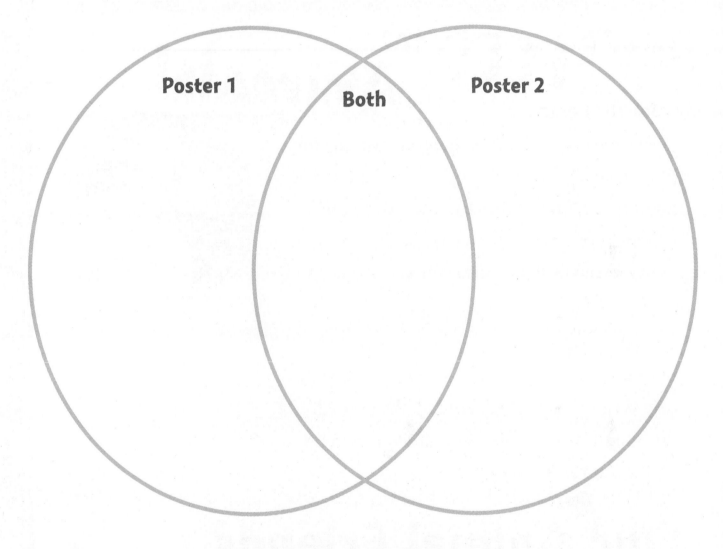

Poster 1　　　Both　　　Poster 2

▶ **Talk** What do you learn about the topic of taking care of planet Earth from comparing and contrasting the posters?

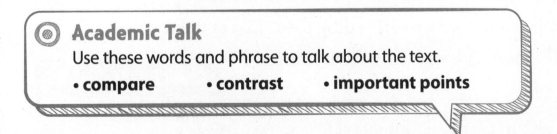

Academic Talk
Use these words and phrase to talk about the text.
- **compare**　　- **contrast**　　- **important points**

　　　Lesson 20 Comparing and Contrasting Two Texts

Don't FEED the Animals!

by Marvin Reinhart

1   Have you ever seen a chipmunk begging for food from a person? Many people might want to give the chipmunk a piece of their snack. But please don't! If we want to have healthy wild animals, then we can't give animals people food.

2   People food can make wild animals sick. It also teaches them to need people to live. Instead of finding their own food, the animals learn to beg. When people aren't around, the animals don't know what to do. They forget how to live off the land around them.

Our Animal Friends

by Jerry Lemto

1   We need to take care of our animals. One way to keep animals safe is not to feed them. Feeding them makes them come back for more. It keeps them from finding their own food.

2   Another way to keep our animals safe is to be careful when driving. Many animals are killed each year by people driving too fast.

> **Close Reader Habits**
>
> **Underline** a sentence in each passage that tells an important point.

Explore How do you compare and contrast the most important points in two texts on the same topic?

Both articles are about animals. I will think about how they are alike and how they are different.

▶ **Think**

1 Use the Venn diagram below to compare and contrast the most important points in the passages.

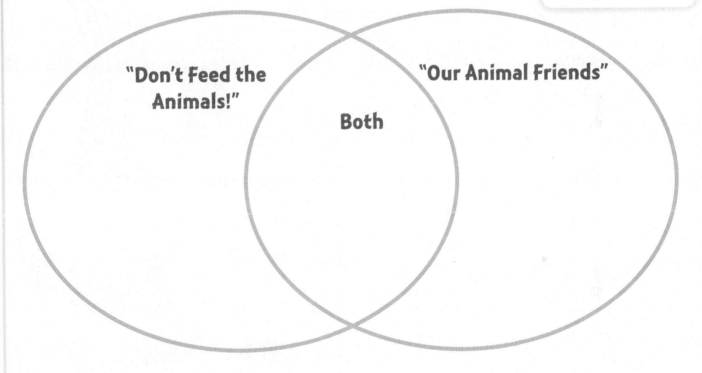

"Don't Feed the Animals!"   Both   "Our Animal Friends"

▶ **Talk**

2 What are the most important points in each passage? Use the information in the Venn diagram to talk about which points are the same in both passages and which are different.

▶  **Write**

3 **Short Response** What is an important point in "Our Animal Friends" that is not in "Don't Feed the Animals!"? Write your answer in the space on page 332.

HINT Look back at the sentences you underlined in both passages.

TURN On the TAP

BY MARISA WOLLCOT

1   Turn on the tap, and out pours fresh, clean water. But where does it come from? In many places, water is pumped from lakes and rivers or from under the ground to wells or to treatment plants. There, it is cleaned to make it safe to drink. Then pipes carry clean water into our homes.

2   Water is important to people— we need it to live! To stay healthy, we drink it every day. We also use it to get clean and to wash away germs. We think there will always be plenty of water when we need it, but that may not be true.

3   In the past, people wasted water. Water was polluted with harmful things, such as garbage and oil.

4   We must protect our water. To make sure we have fresh water in the future, everyone must help today. So be sure to use water wisely!

Close Reader Habits

Why does the author think water is important? **Underline** a sentence that tells why water is important.

Fresh Water

by Seamus Langworthy

1   Fresh water is more precious than gold. Without it, Earth wouldn't have plants, animals, or people. We should always treat water with care.

2   But we put harmful things into our water. Dirty water from homes and factories flows from pipes into rivers. Ships dump garbage and oil into lakes.

3   Cities clean this dirty water. They add things that kill the harmful germs. Now the water that comes from the tap is safe to drink.

4   Keeping water pure is a big job, but you can help! The less water we use, the better. Take shorter showers. Don't leave the tap running when you don't need to. Don't throw garbage into rivers or lakes. If you see garbage, throw it away. Help keep our water pure and safe for everyone to enjoy.

Close Reader Habits

What does the author think people can do to protect water? **Underline** a sentence that tells something people can do to protect water.

▶ Think

1 This question has two parts. Answer Part A. Then answer Part B.

> Both articles are about water. I wonder what each author thinks about this topic.

Part A
What is the most important point in paragraph 2 of "Turn On the Tap"?

- **A** People need water to live.
- **B** We drink water every day.
- **C** Water washes away germs.
- **D** We may not always have enough water.

Part B
Write the sentences from the article that helped you find the answer to Part A.

_____

_____

_____

2 Which important point is in both articles?

- **A** Water comes from the oceans.
- **B** There will always be enough clean water.
- **C** We must protect our water.
- **D** Ships dump garbage into lakes.

3 Which important point is in "Fresh Water" but not in "Turn On the Tap"?

   A   We should use water carefully.

   B   Water is cleaned to make it safe to drink.

   C   People put harmful things into water.

   D   Everyone can help keep water safe.

4 Circle **three** things from the list below that the author of "Fresh Water" says we can do to keep our water pure.

   A   Don't throw garbage into rivers and lakes.

   B   Don't leave the tap running when you don't need to.

   C   Only drink water from the tap.

   D   Close down factories that send dirty water into rivers.

   E   Take shorter showers.

▶ Talk

5 What are both articles mostly about? How are they different? How are they the same? Work with your partner to fill in the Venn diagram on page 333.

▶ Write

6 **Short Response** Use the information from your Venn diagram to describe how the two articles are alike and different. Write your answer in the space on page 333.

> **HINT** Organize your writing to show how the articles are alike and different.

Write Use the space below to write your answer to the question on page 327.

Don't FEED the Animals!

Our Animal Friends

> **HINT** Look back at the sentences you underlined in both passages.

3 **Short Response** What is an important point in "Our Animal Friends" that is not in "Don't Feed the Animals!"?

_____

_____

_____

_____

_____

_____

_____

Check Your Writing

☐ Did you read the question carefully?

☐ Can you say the question in your own words?

☐ Did you use proof from the text in your answer?

☐ Are your ideas in a good, clear order?

☐ Did you answer in full sentences?

☐ Did you check your spelling, capital letters, and periods?

> Don't forget to check your writing.

5 Use the Venn diagram below to organize your ideas.

"Turn On the Tap"   Both   "Fresh Water"

 Write Use the space below to write your answer to the question on page 331.

6 **Short Response** Use the information from your Venn diagram to describe how the two article are alike and different.

> **HINT** Organize your writing to show how the articles are alike and different.

_____

_____

_____

_____

_____

_____

▶ **Read**

Genre: **Social Studies Article**

WORDS TO KNOW
As you read, look inside, around, and beyond these words to figure out what they mean.

- **trash**
- **landfills**
- **recycle**

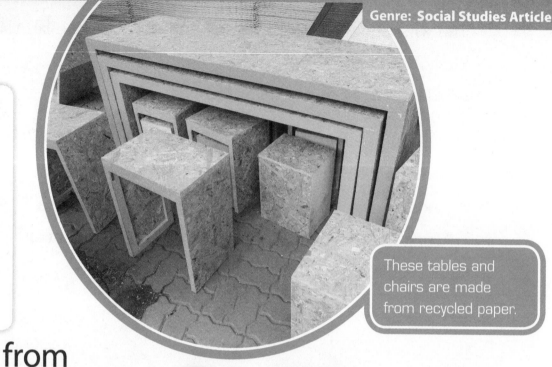

These tables and chairs are made from recycled paper.

from
Recycle That!

by Fay Robinson

1   Bottles, cans, mail, magazines, boxes, bags. We throw out a lot of trash! Everything we throw away came from somewhere. The paper products we use are made from trees. Thousands and thousands of trees are cut down each day to make the paper we use.

2   Fields and hills are dug up to get sand to make glass, and metals to make cans. The plastics we use are made with oil pumped from deep inside the earth.

3   Each time we take something from the earth, we change the earth. The ways we change it are not always good for us, or for wild animals.

4   And where does all our trash go? Most of it goes into land set aside just for trash. But we throw out so much trash that our landfills are filling up. Soon there won't be any more room!

5   By using and throwing away so many things, we have created a big problem. What can you do to help? Recycle!

6   When something is recycled, all or part of it is used again. Many towns and cities have special programs for recycling. Each home gets a special container for items to be recycled.

7   Often, cans, bottles, and newspapers can be recycled. In some places, magazines and plastic bottles can be recycled, too.

8   Can you see why it's smart to recycle? Things that would have been wasted can be made into something useful instead! Each time you recycle one can, bottle, or newspaper, you help the earth a little bit.

9   So recycle that! It's easy!

Elephant art made from plastic bottles!

Genre: Science Article

Turning Trash into Treasure

by Ron Fridell

WORDS TO KNOW

As you read, look inside, around, and beyond these words to figure out what they mean.

- **waste**
- **scraps**
- **cycle**

1   When was the last time you threw away a banana peel? An apple core? A piece of paper? Maybe you could have recycled them instead.

2   When we recycle things, we turn them into new things to use again. From old newspapers, we make new paper. From old cans and empty bottles, we make new ones. Recycling can keep our landfills from getting too full. If we aren't careful, we may run out of room.

3   Composting is another way to recycle. It is a great way to turn food and yard waste into good, rich soil. The soil helps grow new things.

4   To make compost, you need fruit and vegetable scraps. You also need leaves, grass, and soil. Put all these things in a big wooden box. Then add some water and stir. Finally, cover the box.

5   After a few weeks, everything in the compost box starts to rot and break down. The tiniest living things in nature help break them down.

6   After a few more weeks, everything will have turned into rich soil. People use compost in their gardens to help plants and flowers grow.

7   Composting shows us how nature is a cycle. Things grow. Then they die. Finally, they become soil and help new things grow.

8   By recycling things we no longer need, we create new things. We also take better care of the earth.

Think Use what you learned by reading the articles to respond to the following questions.

1. This question has two parts. First, answer Part A. Then answer Part B.

Part A
Based on both articles, which sentence about landfills is true?

A Landfills are a good solution to the trash problem.

B Landfills will never get too full.

C Landfills are safe places to dispose of trash.

D Landfills are not the best way to get rid of trash.

Part B
Write a sentence from each article that helped you find the answer to Part A.

Sentence from "Turning Trash into Treasure"

_____

_____

Sentence from "from *Recycle That!*"

_____

_____

2 Which one of the words and definitions below is the correct meaning of the word "container" found in these sentences from "from *Recycle That!*"?

> **Many towns and cities have special programs for recycling. Each home gets a special container for items to be recycled.**

A **plan** thinking of how to do something before you do it

B **box** something that holds things inside of it

C **area** an open place or space

D **direction** something you follow or a way to go

 Write

Compare and contrast the most important points in the articles. What points are the same? What are two ways the information about recycling in "Turning Trash into Treasure" is different from the information in "from *Recycle That!*"?

3 **Plan Your Response** Reread the two articles. What important points does each writer include about recycling? Underline these important points in both articles. Then make a Venn diagram to compare and contrast them.

4 **Write an Extended Response** Compare and contrast the most important points in the articles. What points are the same? What are two ways the information about recycling in "Turning Trash into Treasure" is **different** from the information in "from *Recycle That!*"?

_____

_____

_____

_____

_____

_____

_____

_____

_____

_____

_____

_____

_____

Learning Target

How does comparing and contrasting the most important points in two texts on the same topic help you learn more about the topic?

_____

_____

_____

▶ **Read**

Read the science articles. Then answer the questions that follow.

Spacesuits and Spaceships

by Ron Fridell

1   What can you see at Space Center Houston? Why, exhibits of course! My favorite is the Astronaut Gallery. It shows the spacesuits that astronauts wear. Why must they wear them?

2   These space travelers must wear a spacesuit when they go outside the ship. The astronauts test new equipment and do experiments. There is no oxygen in outer space. The suit gives them air to breathe.

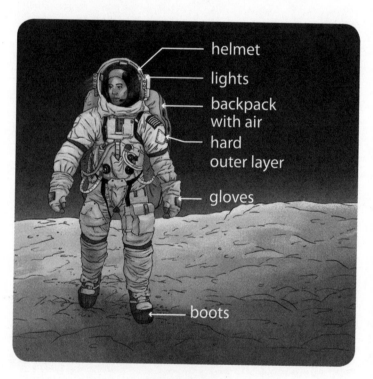

Spacesuit

3   It also protects them from the heat and cold. In the sunlight, it can be as hot as 250 degrees! In shadow, it can be as cold as minus 250 degrees! A spacesuit is like a little spaceship. It keeps the astronaut safe.

4   Now let's take a look at the Apollo 17 command module. This is part of the ship that carried three astronauts to the Moon and back in 1972. One of them stayed inside it, circling the Moon. The other two flew down to explore the Moon's surface.

5   Notice that the diagram on this page shows a place at the top for parachutes. When the ship returned to Earth, the parachutes helped slow it down. It landed in the ocean with the crew safe and sound.

6   Finally, let's look at the *Saturn Five* rocket in Rocket Park. The ship is set down on its side, so that you can walk all around it. The rocket is as long as a football field. It weighs more than six million pounds. A rocket just like it took the Apollo 17 astronauts up into space, and then fell back to Earth.

7   There's lots more to see at the Space Center. And there's lots more to learn.

Apollo 17 Command Module

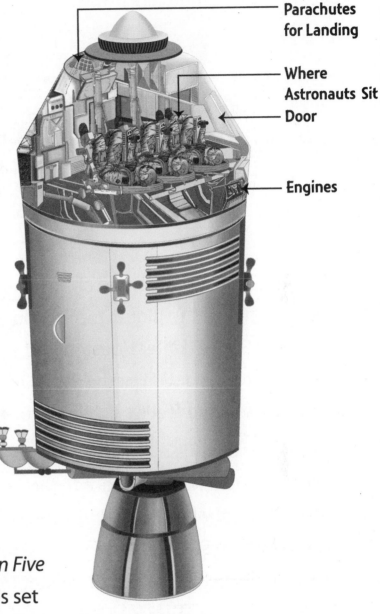

Parachutes for Landing

Where Astronauts Sit

Door

Engines

Genre: Science Article

Space Center HOUSTON

by Emily Paul

1   Have you ever dreamed of being an astronaut? If so, you might want to plan a trip to Houston, Texas. You can visit Space Center Houston and the Johnson Space Center. Start your visit at the Blast Off Theater. Here, you can see and feel what it is like to lift off into space!

2   Not far away is the Johnson Space Center. This is where people work on space flights. You might get to see the room where men and women help the astronauts in space. Maybe you will see some astronauts getting ready for a flight.

3   Be sure to look for the Astronaut Gallery. This big room is filled with real spacesuits. The walls have pictures of people who have flown in space. Part of the Gallery is called Living in Space. It shows how astronauts work, eat, and sleep in space.

This astronaut is training underwater at the Johnson Space Center.

4   Moving around in space is very different from the way we move on Earth. Astronauts can float inside the space station. They must learn how to safely move without bumping into things.

5   Even eating and sleeping are different on a space station. Astronauts need to hang on to what they are eating or it will float away! Most space food is kept in plastic containers. Drinks come in sealed pouches and are sipped with a straw. When it's time to go to bed, astronauts climb into small sleeping bags and tie themselves in. This is so they don't float around while they are sleeping!

6   Before you leave, don't forget to visit the Kids' Space Place. It is a giant inside playground. You can pretend you are flying the space shuttle. Or you can imagine that you live on the space station. It is the perfect way to end your busy day.

Astronaut Chris Hadfield is juggling some tomatoes on the International Space Station. Can you guess why they are floating?

▶ **Think**

1 Look at the diagram of the Apollo 17 command module on page 341. Which sentence from "Spacesuits and Spaceships" tells more about this diagram?

    A "The astronauts test new equipment and do experiments."

    B "This is part of the ship that carried three astronauts to the Moon and back in 1972."

    C "Finally, let's look at the *Saturn Five* rocket in Rocket Park."

    D "The ship is set down on its side, so that you can walk all around it."

2 What does the diagram on page 341 show that is **not** told about in the article?

    A It shows that the command module had parachutes for landing.

    B It shows that the astronauts floated inside the command module.

    C It shows that the command module had its own engines.

    D It shows that the astronauts wore spacesuits outside the command module.

3 In paragraph 3 of "Spacesuits and Spaceships," the author makes the point that a spacesuit is like a little spaceship. What reason from the article **best** explains this point?

    A "Why must they wear them?"

    B "It also protects them from the heat and cold."

    C "In the sunlight, it can be as hot as 250 degrees!"

    D "In shadow, it can be as cold as minus 250 degrees!"

4 Choose **two** sentences from "Spacesuits and Spaceships" that the diagram of a spacesuit on page 340 helps to explain.

    A "These space travelers must wear a spacesuit when they go outside the ship."

    B "The astronauts test new equipment and do experiments."

    C "There is no oxygen in outer space."

    D "The suit gives them air to breathe."

    E "In the sunlight, it can be as hot as 250 degrees!"

5 Underline the sentence below that **best** explains what is happening in the picture on page 344.

   Even eating and sleeping are different on a space station. Astronauts need to hang on to what they are eating or it will float away! Most space food is kept in plastic containers. Drinks come in sealed pouches and are sipped with a straw. When it's time to go to bed, astronauts climb into small sleeping bags and tie themselves in. This is so they don't float around while they are sleeping!

6 This question has two parts. First, answer Part A. Then answer Part B.

Part A

In paragraphs 4 and 5 of "Space Center Houston," what key point does the author make about floating inside the space station?

(A) Astronauts must learn to move safely.

B Astronauts must always wear a spacesuit.

C Astronauts must drink from a straw.

D Astronauts must sleep in sleeping bags.

Part B

What reason does the author give to explain the key point she makes about floating inside the space station?

The reason is that they have to learn to move without bumping into things

7 In "Space Center Houston," the author makes the point that readers should visit the Astronaut Gallery. Choose **two** details from the article that support this point.

- **A** The gallery is filled with food and drink.
- **B** The gallery lets you pretend to fly a space shuttle.
- **C** The gallery shows how astronauts work.
- **D** The gallery tells how to get to the space station.
- **E** The gallery has real spacesuits.

8 Read the sentences from "Space Center Houston" below.

Most space food is kept in plastic containers. Drinks come in sealed pouches and are sipped with a straw.

Which choice **best** tells what "sealed pouches" are?

- **A** covered drinking glasses
- **B** tightly closed bags
- **C** holes for straws
- **D** large pockets

9 Which important point is in "Space Center Houston" but **not** in "Spacesuits and Spaceships"?

- **A** People work on real space flights at the Johnson Space Center.
- **B** Astronauts went to the Moon in the Apollo 17 command module.
- **C** Astronauts do experiments when they go outside the ship.
- **D** The *Saturn Five* rocket in Rocket Park is as long as a football field.

10 Which important point is in **both** articles?

- **A** Parachutes help slow down a returning spaceship.
- **B** Real spacesuits can be found in the Astronaut Gallery.
- **C** The *Saturn Five* rocket weighs more than six million pounds.
- **D** Space can be as cold as minus 250 degrees.

Write

Extended Response Compare and contrast the **most** important points in the articles about living in space. What points are the same? What are ways the information about living in space in "Spacesuits and Spaceships" is **different** from the information in "Space Center Houston"?

11 | **Plan Your Response** Reread the two articles. What important points does each writer include about living in space? Underline these important points in both articles. Then fill in the chart below to compare and contrast them.

Important Points About the Way Astronauts Live in Space

Spacesuits and Spaceships	Space Center Houston
Point 1:	Point 1:
Point 2:	Point 2:
Point 3:	Point 3:

12 **Write an Extended Response** Compare and contrast the **most** important points in the articles about living in space. What points are the same? What are ways the information about living in space in "Spacesuits and Spaceships" is **different** from the information in "Space Center Houston"? Use information in your chart in your answer.

_____

_____

_____

_____

_____

_____

_____

_____

_____

_____

_____

_____

_____

_____

Integration of Knowledge and Ideas in Literature

Sometimes, you can read the same story in different books. For example, did you know there are many different stories that tell the story of Cinderella? In China, Cinderella is called Yeh-Shen. Instead of a fairy godmother, Yeh-Shen is helped by a magic fish.

In this unit, you will use the pictures that go with stories to help you better understand the characters and what happens to them. You will also look at ways different people in different places have told the same stories.

✓ Self Check

Before starting this unit, check off the skills you know below. As you complete each lesson, see how many more skills you can check off!

I can:	Before this unit	After this unit
explain how pictures in a story help me understand a story's characters.	☐	☐
explain how pictures in a story help me understand a story's setting.	☐	☐
explain how pictures in a story help me understand a story's plot.	☐	☐
compare and contrast the same story told by different authors.	☐	☐
compare and contrast the same story from different cultures.	☐	☐

page 360

page 362

page 366

page 377

page 378

page 384

👥 **Introduction**

LAFS.2.RL.3.7 Use information gained from the illustrations and words in a print or digital text to demonstrate understanding of its characters, setting, or plot.

Lesson 21
Connecting Words and Pictures

 **Learning Target**

Use information from the pictures and words in a story to help you better understand the characters, setting, and plot.

▶ **Read** Words and pictures, or **illustrations**, work together to help you better understand what happens in a story. They can give you details about the **setting,** or where the story takes place. Words and pictures help you know what the **characters** are like. They also help you understand the **plot,** or what is happening in the story.

Read the sentences and look at the illustrations. What do the pictures tell you that the words do not?

Picture 1

"I don't *want* to go on the roller coaster," said Allison.

"Oh, come on," said her mom. "It'll be fun!"

Picture 2

As it turned out, her mom was right. Sort of.

▶ **Think** Look again at the pictures and words. Finish the chart to show what each adds to the story.

	What the Sentences Tell	**What the Pictures Show**
Picture 1	Allison doesn't want to go on the ride.	
Picture 2	Allison's mom was partly right.	

▶ **Talk** Think about the cartoon again. How do the words and pictures work together to help you understand what happens?

◎ **Academic Talk**
Use these words to talk about the text.
- **illustrations** - **characters** - **setting** - **plot**

▶ **Read**

Mr. March and the Moose

by Wendell Riley

1   Mr. March could not find his glasses anywhere. He had searched his whole house, and he'd even poked around his backyard. When he came inside, he hung his hat and coat on the coat rack.

Picture 1

2   "Where could those glasses be?" he muttered. "I can't see three feet without them! And I was so hoping to spot that moose everyone has been talking about."

3   "Excuse me, sir," a shy voice said. "I believe your glasses are in your shirt pocket."

4   Mr. March jumped! Who had said that? But he reached in his pocket and there were his glasses! When he put them on, he realized he had not hung his hat and coat on the coat rack after all.

Picture 2

Close Reader Habits

Circle details in the pictures that aren't in the sentences.

Explore How do the words and pictures work together to help make "Mr. March and the Moose" a funny story?

▶ **Think**

> I need to look at each picture, read the words, and then look at each picture again.

1 Look again at the pictures and words. Finish the chart to show what each adds to the story.

	What the Sentences Tell	What the Pictures Show
Picture 1	• Mr. March can't find his glasses.	
Picture 2	• Someone tells Mr. March where his glasses are.	

▶ **Talk**

2 Mr. March says he's hoping to see a moose. How does Picture 1 help make this line from the story funny?

▶  **Write**

3 **Short Response** What does Mr. March find out once he puts his glasses on? How do the words and pictures help you understand this? Write your answer in the space on page 358.

> **HINT** Where did Mr. March hang his hat and coat?

> Read

Fast Learner

by Julie Barnes

1   Thunder had a serious problem. He couldn't seem to train his owner, Penny, though he knew she was trying hard. His friend Pepper gave him a book called *How to Train Your Owner.* She said she'd found it very useful with her own girl. The first chapter looked helpful: "How to Walk Your Person."

2   That night, Thunder brought Penny his leash, which meant that it was time for their daily walk. As usual, though, Penny walked much too fast, leaving Thunder no time to search for good smells.

3   So Thunder did what the book told him to do. First, he sat down and dug in his paws. Penny stopped. Then Thunder stood up and started walking by her side. He walked at a nice, slow pace.

4   Penny soon was walking ahead again, so Thunder repeated what he had learned. This time, it worked! Penny walked slowly at Thunder's side. "Good girl!" thought Thunder, rewarding her with a tail wag.

5   It took Thunder three weeks to finish the book. After a lot of practice, Thunder had a well-trained owner!

Close Reader Habits

How do the picture and words help you understand that this story is a fantasy? **Circle** something in the picture and **underline** the sentences that show this is a fantasy.

► **Think**

1 What is Thunder's problem?

    A   His person doesn't want to be trained.

    B   He doesn't like going on walks.

    C   His friend Pepper didn't want to help him.

    D   His person was hard to teach.

> I'll look at the picture again and reread the story to find out how Thunder trained Penny.

2 What part of the story is the picture showing?

    A   how Thunder learns to train Penny

    B   the problem Thunder was having with Penny

    C   how Penny and Thunder look after training

    D   how Thunder rewarded Penny

► **Talk**

3 Look closely at the picture again. What details in the picture help make the story funny? Talk with a partner about it.

► **Write**

4 **Short Response** What is funny about the training that goes on in this story? Explain your answer, using details from the story and picture. Write your answer in the space on page 359.

> **HINT** What can Thunder and Pepper do that real dogs can't?

Write Use the space below to write your answer to the question on page 355.

Mr. March and the Moose

3 **Short Response** What does Mr. March find out once he puts his glasses on? How do the words and pictures help you understand this?

> **HINT** Where did Mr. March hang his hat and coat?

_____

_____

_____

_____

_____

_____

_____

Don't forget to check your writing.

Write Use the space below to write your answer to the question on page 357.

Fast Learner

4 **Short Response** What is funny about the training that goes on in this story? Explain your answer, using details from the story and picture.

HINT What can Thunder and Pepper do that real dogs can't?

_____

_____

_____

_____

_____

_____

_____

Check Your Writing

☐ Did you read the question carefully?

☐ Can you say the question in your own words?

☐ Did you use proof from the text in your answer?

☐ Are your ideas in a good, clear order?

☐ Did you answer in full sentences?

☐ Did you check your spelling, capital letters, and periods?

▶ **Read**

Gu Dong is Coming!

Based on a traditional Chinese folktale by Xu Li

WORDS TO KNOW
As you read, look inside, around, and beyond these words to figure out what they mean.
- **papaya**
- **dared**
- **trembled**

1   Rabbit White nibbled grass by the pond where a tall papaya tree stood. Suddenly, Rabbit White heard *Gu Dong!* He jumped so high his ears brushed the branches of the papaya tree.

2   "A monster is coming!" Rabbit White shouted, hopping away as fast as he could. He dared not even look back. "A . . . a . . . a Gu Dong is coming!"

3   He jumped over brooks and logs. He even bounced over Monkey, who was eating a banana on a fallen log.

4   "What's your hurry? Who's Gu Dong?" Monkey jumped from the log and dashed after Rabbit White.

5   Rabbit White said, "A monster, big and scary. We must call all of our friends."

6   "Gu Dong is coming!" they shouted as they ran. Soon they bumped into Fox.

GU DONG!

7   "What's your hurry? Who's Gu Dong?" Fox asked.

8   "I'm sure he is a monster with three big red eyes!"
Rabbit White said.

9   "With the biggest red eye in his forehead," Monkey added.

10 Fox trembled when he pictured the fearsome Gu Dong.

11 "Stay with us. You will be safe," Rabbit White promised.

12 So Fox and Monkey dashed after Rabbit White.

13 "Gu Dong is coming!" they shouted.

14 Before long, Spotted Deer, Bear, and Tiger had joined them.
"Gu Dong is coming!" they shouted together.

15 Lion walked slowly through the deep grass.
"Who's this Gu Dong?" he asked.

16 "He is a monster," said Rabbit White.

17 "He is huge," Bear said.

18 "He will eat us all," cried Tiger.

19 "He has three big red eyes," Monkey chattered.

20 "Who has seen Gu Dong?" Lion asked, smiling.

21 The animals looked at Rabbit White. He said, "I heard him by the pond."

22 "Let's find out who this Gu Dong is," said Lion.

23 So Rabbit White led Monkey, Fox, Spotted Deer, Bear, Tiger, and Lion back to the pond. But no one was there. Only a ripe papaya floated on the water.

24 "I know I heard Gu Dong!" Tears ran down Rabbit White's face. Just then, another ripe papaya fell into the pond. *Gu Dong!*

25 "Aaaugh!" Rabbit White screamed and then started laughing. "It's only the papaya!" he cried out with joy.

26 Lion picked up a papaya and broke it open. Then they all enjoyed a papaya lunch at the edge of the pond.

▶ **Think** Use what you learned from reading the selection to respond to these questions.

1 On page 360, what **two** important details can you see in the picture that are not in the text?

    A that other animals live near Rabbit White

    B that the story takes place in the jungle

    C that a papaya makes the sound that scares Rabbit White

    D that Monkey also hears the sound of Gu Dong

    E that a monster is hiding in the trees above Rabbit White

2 This question has two parts. First, answer Part A. Then answer Part B.

Part A
What does the picture on page 361 show?

    A what the Gu Dong really looks like

    B what the animals think Gu Dong looks like

    C what Rabbit White saw by the pond

    D what Lion knows about Gu Dong

Part B
Write **two** details from the story that match what is shown in the picture.

"With the biggest red eye on his forhead, He is huge.

3 Which sentence **best** shows that Lion knows Gu Dong is not a monster?

    A "Lion walked slowly through the deep grass."

    B "'Who has seen Gu Dong?' Lion asked, smiling."

    C "'Let's find out who this Gu Dong is,' said Lion."

    D "Lion picked up a papaya and broke it open."

4 Read this sentence from paragraph 10.

> Fox trembled when he pictured the fearsome Gu Dong.

After breaking the word "fearsome" into two parts, what would you say it means?

    A very ugly

    B scary

    C colorful

    D huge

Write Many stories are told to teach a lesson. Think about the lesson that "Gu Dong Is Coming!" teaches.

5 **Plan Your Response** Write what you think the lesson of the story is. Make a list of details from the text and the pictures that help teach that lesson.

6 **Write an Extended Response** Explain how "Gu Dong Is Coming!" teaches a lesson. Use details from the text and the pictures to support your ideas.

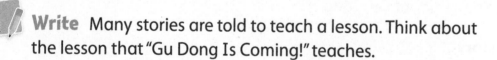

It teaches to check first before saying any thing is true.

Learning Target

How can using both words and pictures when you read help you better understand a story?

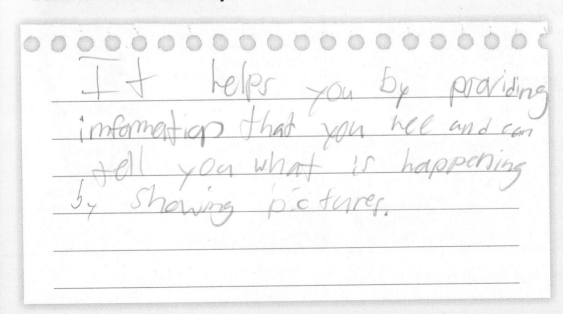

It helps you by providing imformation that you hel and can tell you what is happening by showing pictures.

🐾 **Introduction**

LAFS.2.RL.3.9 Compare and contrast two or more versions of the same story (e.g., Cinderella stories) by different authors or from different cultures.

Lesson 22
Comparing and Contrasting Stories

Learning Target

Reading two versions of a story will help you see how writers can tell the same story in different ways.

▶ **Read** When you **compare** stories, you find ways they are alike. When you **contrast** stories, you find ways they are different. Sometimes two stories have mostly the same plot. But they may have different characters or settings. These are called **versions** of a story. Different versions of the same story are often told in different countries.

Look at the two pictures below. They are from two versions of the story "Little Red Riding Hood." How are they alike and different?

Little Red Riding Hood

Pretty Salma

▶ **Think** Look at the two pictures again. What is the same, and what is different? Fill in the *Venn diagram* below to compare and contrast the two pictures.

"Little Red Riding Hood"   Both   "Pretty Salma"

▶ **Talk** Share your chart with your classmates. Tell how the two pictures are alike and different.

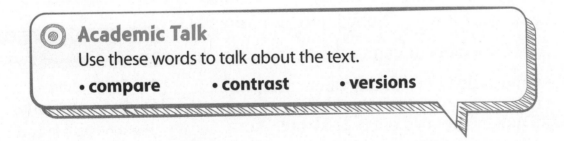

◎ **Academic Talk**
Use these words to talk about the text.

- **compare**   • **contrast**   • **versions**

The Turtle and the Rabbit   from Aesop

1   "No one in all the forest is faster than I am," Rabbit boasted to the other animals one day. "And I can prove it! Who wants to race me?"

2   None of the animals accepted Rabbit's challenge, except for Turtle. "I will race you," he said, rather slowly.

3   "You?" Rabbit said. "What a joke! I'll be at the finish line before you've even started!"

4   As soon as the race began, Rabbit hopped away at great speed. After a while, he was so far ahead that he decided to take a nap. Turtle, on the other hand, did not stop for a minute. He just kept going, and going, and going. When Rabbit finally woke up, he saw Turtle nearing the finish line. Rabbit ran as fast as he could, but Turtle won!

5   "Steady wins the race," Turtle said, rather slowly, as always.

The Fox and the Snail   after Aesop

1   Fox asked Snail to run a race with him to the next town. Fox took off running, but then he decided to take a nap. When Snail saw the sleeping fox, he climbed into his bushy tail. When Fox woke up, he ran to the town's gate. He turned and called out, "Snail, where are you?"

2   Snail quietly dropped out of Fox's tail. "I'm already here!" Snail said from behind him. "What took you so long?"

Close Reader Habits

Circle the main characters. **Underline** the sentences in each story that tell how one animal wins the race.

Explore **How are the two stories alike and different?**

Think

To compare the stories, I'll look at the characters and the plot.

1 Look back at what you underlined and circled. Then complete the *Venn diagram* to show how the two stories are alike and different.

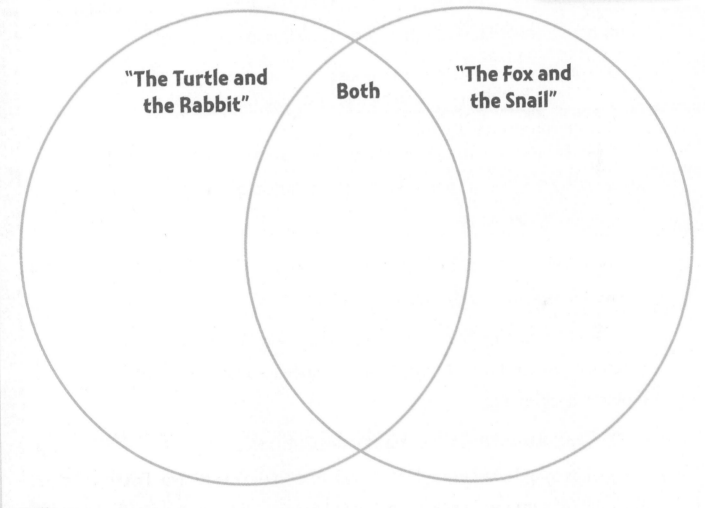

"The Turtle and the Rabbit"

Both

"The Fox and the Snail"

Talk

2 How is Rabbit like Fox? How are they different?

HINT First, look at the diagram to help you answer.

Write

3 **Short Response** The slower animal wins in both races. Tell what each one does to win. Write your answer in the space on page 374.

The Three Little Pigs

a folktale from England

1   Long ago, three little pigs grew up and left their family home. One built a straw house, one built a wood house, and one built a brick house.

2   One day, a wolf found the straw house. "Let me in, little pig!" he called.

3   "I won't!" said the first pig.

4   "Then I'll huff, I'll puff, and I'll blow your house in!" cried the wolf. That's just what he did, and the house fell apart. The little pig squeaked and ran to his brother's wood house.

5   But the wolf soon found the wood house, too. "Let me in, little pigs!"

6   "Never!" yelled the two brothers.

7   "Then I'll huff, I'll puff, and I'll blow your house in!" The wolf blew hard, and the house fell down. The two brothers squeaked and ran to their brother's brick house.

8   The wolf followed them. "Let me in, little pigs!"

9   "We won't!" they all cried.

10 "Then I'll huff, I'll puff, and I'll blow your house in," the wolf growled.

11 But this time he couldn't blow it down! So he crawled up on the roof and slid down the chimney. He fell into a pot of boiling water the little pigs had put in the fireplace.

12 The wolf never bothered the pigs again.

Close Reader Habits

Who are the characters in this story? **Circle** the characters in this story. **Underline** what happens to the three houses.

The Three Geese  a folktale from Italy

1   Once upon a time, three geese built a straw house together. But the oldest goose decided to keep the house for herself. "Go away!" she said to her sisters, and she locked the door behind them.

2   The two younger sisters built a second house of hay. Then the middle goose decided to keep it. "Go away!" she told her sister, and she locked the door behind her. The youngest goose went off sadly and built her own house from stones.

3   A wolf came upon the flimsy straw house and, laughing, he blew it down. The oldest goose ran to the middle goose's house. Her sister sighed but allowed her in.

4   Unfortunately, the wolf was close behind. With one breath, he destroyed the house. The two geese ran to their sister's stone house, and she welcomed them in.

5   The wolf soon arrived at the house. He tried to blow it down, but the stone house didn't fall. Then the youngest goose had an idea. She began cooking soup.

6   "Would you like a taste?" she asked the wolf.

7   "I would!" said the wolf.

8   The goose opened a window and threw the hot soup at the wolf. He ran away howling, leaving the three geese to live happily ever after—together.

Close Reader Habits

Who are the characters in this story? **Circle** the characters in the story. **Underline** what happens to the wolf.

Think

1 Fill in the chart to show how the stories are the same and different.

> I can use a chart to help me organize what happens in each story.

	"The Three Little Pigs"	"The Three Geese"
Who are the main characters?		
What are their houses made of?		
Who causes a problem?		
Which house stays up?		
How is the wolf stopped?		

2 Which **two** sentences **best** tell how the plots of the stories are alike?

  A   Both stories are about animals who get locked out of their houses.

  B   Both stories are about animals who build houses of straw, wood, and stone.

  C   Both stories tell about three animals who are visited by a mean wolf.

  D   Both stories tell about how a wolf gets tricked.

  E   Both stories are about a wolf who wants someone else's house.

3 Which sentence **best** tells how the three geese are different from the three pigs?

  A   The pigs build their houses, but the geese do not.

  B   The two older geese are selfish, but the three pigs are not.

  C   The pigs are afraid of the wolf, but the geese are not.

  D   The geese build strong houses, but the pigs do not.

▶ **Talk**

4 What lesson do you think the older geese learn from how their youngest sister acted? Talk about your ideas with a partner.

▶ **Write**

5 **Short Response** How are the endings of the two stories alike? How are they different? Write your answer in the space on page 375.

> **HINT** Think about what happens to the wolf in each story.

Write Use the space below to write your answer to the question on page 369.

The **Turtle** and the **Rabbit**

The **Fox** and the **Snail**

3 **Short Response** The slower animal wins in both races. Tell what each one does to win.

_____

_____

_____

_____

_____

_____

_____

Don't forget to check your writing.

Write Use the space below to write your answer to the question on page 373.

The Three Little Pigs   The Three Geese

5 **Short Response** How are the endings of the two stories alike? How are they different?

> **HINT** Think about what happens to the wolf in each story.

_____

_____

_____

_____

_____

_____

_____

Check Your Writing

☐ Did you read the question carefully?

☐ Can you say the question in your own words?

☐ Did you use proof from the text in your answer?

☐ Are your ideas in a good, clear order?

☐ Did you answer in full sentences?

☐ Did you check your spelling, capital letters, and periods?

THE UGLY TRUCKLING

by David Gordon

WORDS TO KNOW
As you read, look inside, around, and beyond these words to figure out what they mean.

• beams
• haul
• bale
• propellers
• reflection

1   Way out west, a mother truck admired her new trucklings. She smiled at their big, round wheels and their strong, flat beds.

2   But one of the trucklings was not like her brothers and sisters. This truckling's wheels were small and narrow. She didn't have a strong, flat bed. To make matters worse, two strange beams stuck out from the sides of her body.

3   The next morning the little trucklings followed their mother, carrying rocks and bricks and wood in their little truck beds.

4   But the ugly truckling could barely haul a small bale of hay or pull a log. All the other little trucklings laughed at her. "Why do you have three wheels instead of four?" asked one of her brothers.

5   "You'll never be a good truck," said another brother. The ugly truckling was very sad. She was afraid he was right.

6   So late one night, when the sky was
black and starless, the ugly truckling sped away.

7   The next morning she met a tractor. "Good morning," said the
ugly truckling. Who are you?"

8   "I'm a tractor," said the tractor.

9   "Am I a tractor, too?"

10   "You're no tractor. Tractors don't have propellers on their noses."

11   "Oh," sighed the ugly truckling. And she sped away. The ugly
truckling looked at her reflection in the pond. Suddenly she heard a
loud roar overhead and looked up.

12   She wasn't an ugly truckling after all. She was a beautiful
airplane. And so she flew away with the other airplanes into a sky
full of stars.

Genre: Folktale

The Ugly Duckling

by Hans Christian Andersen, retold by Nicole Flowers

WORDS TO KNOW

As you read, look inside, around, and beyond these words to figure out what they mean.

- swooped
- stretched

1   Once upon a time, there was a baby duckling who looked nothing like his brothers and sisters. His feet looked like big paddles. His feathers were gray, like old dishwater.

2   The other ducklings at the pond laughed at him. They said that his quack sounded like a broken horn. So one day, the ugly duckling left the pond to find a new home.

3   Soon, the weather grew cold. Each time the duckling saw a bird, he asked, "Am I one of you?" But the birds told him he didn't look anything like them.

4   The winter was long, but finally spring came. One day, the duckling saw a group of beautiful birds. Their feathers were snow white, and their necks were long and graceful.

5   "I know I can't be one of them," the duckling sighed.

6   But one of the birds swooped down to where the duckling sat. "You are a swan, like me," the bird said. "Come with us."

7   The duckling walked over to a puddle of water. That is when he saw that his ugly gray feathers were gone. He was snow white, like the other birds. His neck was long and graceful.

8   And so the duckling, really a swan, stretched out his great wings. He flew into the sky with his new friends.

▶ **Think** Use what you learned from reading the stories to respond to these questions.

1 This question has two parts. First, answer Part A. Then answer Part B.

Part A
Both the ugly truckling and the ugly duckling leave their families. How are their reasons for leaving **alike?**

   A Both find it hard to do their work at home.

   B Both are laughed at by those close to them.

   C Both want to escape the cold winter weather.

   D Both want to make new friends.

Part B
Which **two** sentences from the passages show how the truckling and duckling are alike?

   A "This truckling's wheels were small and narrow."

   B "All the other little trucklings laughed at her."

   C "The duckling walked over to a puddle of water."

   D "The other ducklings at the pond laughed at him."

   E "He was snow white, like the other birds."

2 How is the ugly duckling **different** from the ugly truckling?

   A He is happy with his family.

   B He asks many questions.

   C He likes the way he looks.

   D His looks begin to change.

3 Read paragraph 4 of "The Ugly Duckling."

> The winter was long, but finally spring came. One day, the duckling saw a group of beautiful birds. Their feathers were snow white, and their necks were long and graceful.

What does "graceful" mean in this paragraph?

A gray

B crooked

C beautiful

D strong

 Write What lesson do you learn in both "The Ugly Duckling" and "The Ugly Truckling"?

4 **Plan Your Response** The author of "The Ugly Truckling" wanted to tell the story of "The Ugly Duckling" in a new way. Read both stories again to see how they alike. Make a list of the ways the two stories are the same.

_____

_____

_____

_____

_____

5 **Write an Extended Response** Two versions of a story usually have the same lesson. What lesson do you learn in both "The Ugly Duckling" and "The Ugly Truckling"? Include some of the details that help teach that lesson.

_____

_____

_____

_____

_____

_____

_____

Learning Target

How does reading two versions of a story help you see how writers can tell the same story in different ways?

_____

_____

_____

_____

▶ **Read**

Read the folktales. Then answer the questions that follow.

The Stonecutter

a folktale from Japan

1   Long ago, a man named Toshi lived in Japan. Toshi was a stonecutter. Each day, he went to the mountains with his tools and cut huge blocks of stone to sell. Toshi wasn't rich, but his work made him happy, and he was content with his life.

2   One day, Toshi heard a story about a spirit. People said the spirit granted four wishes to any person. The next day when Toshi went to work, he closed his eyes and said, "Oh, how I wish I were rich!"

3   When he got home that evening, Toshi was astonished to see that he had become rich. His small house was now a beautiful palace!

Lovely, colorful gardens stretched out behind his new home, and a dinner of the finest foods was waiting for him inside. Toshi was excited and happy about his good fortune.

4   When winter came, so did the rain. Toshi thought, "I'm rich, but I'm not strong like the rain. I want to be the rain." Suddenly, Toshi became the rain!

5   He was so strong that his floods destroyed the town. The only things left standing were the mountains. "A mountain is stronger than the rain," said Toshi. "I wish I were a mountain." Almost at once, he became a mountain.

6   One day, a stonecutter came to the mountain. He swung his hammer and took off a huge stone slab. "This man is stronger than a mountain," Toshi cried. "Oh, how I wish I were a man."

7   The spirit granted his last wish, and Toshi returned to his life as a stonecutter. He wasn't rich or strong anymore, but he was happy. He never wished to be anything but a stonecutter again. Being anything else was too much trouble!

Genre: Folktale

The Woodcutter

by Charles Perrault, retold by Eugenie Caldwell

1   Once upon a time, there was an unhappy woodcutter. He was tired of cutting wood and complained about it every day.

2   One morning, he was taking a long walk through the green forest. Suddenly, a large hawk appeared in front of him and said, "Hello!" The woodcutter was very startled, and he jumped back to get a better look at the hawk.

3   The bird said, "Do not be afraid. My name is Horus, and I am king of the sky. I have heard you complaining, and I have come to grant you three wishes. Remember, think carefully before you make your wish." With that, Horus spread his enormous wings and flew away.

4   The woodcutter ran home to tell his wife the good news. But she was wise and said, "We need to think carefully about this."

5   The man agreed and sat down to eat his dinner. He looked at his plate and frowned. Beans again. He said, "I wish I had some chicken."

6   A piece of chicken suddenly appeared on the man's plate.

7   "Oh no! You are a silly man!" yelled his wife. "You have wasted one of our wishes on a chicken!"

8   "I am not silly!" yelled the man. "I am tired of eating your beans. I wish this piece of chicken was hanging from your ear!" he yelled.

9   Suddenly, the piece of chicken was attached to his wife's ear. She screamed in horror and tried to pull the chicken off, but it wouldn't budge.

10   The woodcutter sighed, and said, "I have one wish left. I can wish for money, or I can wish for my wife's happiness."

11   The woodcutter said, "I wish that the piece of chicken would fall off my wife's ear."

12   The chicken fell off, and the woodcutter went back to his wood cutting. He never complained again.

▶ **Think**

1 Which sentence from "The Stonecutter" **best** tells about the picture on page 382?

　　A "Each day, he went to the mountain with his tools and cut huge blocks of stone to sell."

　　B "When he got home that evening, Toshi was astonished to see that he had become rich."

　　C "When winter came, so did the rain."

　　D "The only things left standing were the mountains."

2 What can you tell about Toshi in "The Stonecutter" from both the story and the picture on page 383?

　　A Toshi is angry to be a mountain.

　　B Toshi is excited to be a mountain.

　　C Toshi is unhappy to be a mountain.

　　D Toshi is proud to be a mountain.

3 Underline the word in the sentence from "The Stonecutter" below that gives a clue to the meaning of "content."

　　Toshi wasn't rich, but his work made him happy, and he was <u>content</u> with his life.

4 How does the woodcutter feel when he first meets the hawk? Think about both the picture on page 384 and the story.

　　A peaceful

　　B surprised

　　C lucky

　　D bored

5 What does the picture on page 385 show about what happens after the woodcutter makes his second wish?

    A   It shows why the woodcutter made the wish.

    B   It shows how the chicken falls off the wife's ear.

    C   It shows the woodcutter has decided what to wish for next.

    D   It shows how the wife feels about the woodcutter's wish.

6 This question has two parts. First, answer Part A. Then answer Part B.

Part A
Read the following sentence from "The Woodcutter."

> **She screamed in horror and tried to pull the chicken off, but it wouldn't budge.**

What do the words "it wouldn't budge" mean in this context?

    A   It wouldn't shut.

    B   It wouldn't stick.

    C   It wouldn't move.

    D   It wouldn't stop.

Part B
Underline the phrase in the sentence in Part A that helped you figure out the meaning of "it wouldn't budge."

7 This question has two parts. First, answer Part A. Then answer Part B.

Part A

Which sentence **best** tells how the plots of the stories are **alike**?

    A   Both stories tell about a person who wishes to change into something else.

    B   Both stories tell about a person who gives up his happiness to help someone.

    C   Both stories tell about a person who makes wishes that cause trouble.

    D   Both stories tell about a person who is visited by a strange animal.

Part B

Which **two** sentences from the stories show how their plots are **alike**?

    A   "Toshi was happy and excited about his good fortune."

    B   "He was so strong that his floods destroyed the town."

    C   "Once upon a time, there was an unhappy woodcutter."

    D   "Suddenly, a large hawk appeared in front of him and said, 'Hello!'"

    E   "A piece of chicken suddenly appeared on the man's plate."

8 What is one way the stonecutter and the woodcutter are **alike**?

    A   Both are very unhappy with their work.

    B   Both care about making their wives happy.

    C   Both want to be stronger than they are.

    D   Both make wishes that come true.

9 How are the stonecutter's wishes and the woodcutter's wishes **different**?

    A   The stonecutter makes a careful first wish, but the woodcutter does not.

    B   The stonecutter wishes to be strong, but the woodcutter wishes to be rich.

    C   The stonecutter's wishes help others, but the woodcutter's wishes help himself.

    D   The stonecutter's wishes come true, but the woodcutter's wishes do not come true.

Write

Extended Response What lesson do you learn in both "The Stonecutter" and "The Woodcutter"?

10 **Plan Your Response** Each story tells what happens when someone is given a certain number of wishes. Read both stories again to see what the stonecutter and the woodcutter learn from making their wishes. Use the questions below to list details about their wishes.

What does the stonecutter do with his wishes in "The Stonecutter"?

He wishes for things that he wants. not what he needs

How does the stonecutter feel about his wishes at the end of the story?

That he could of made better wishes

Why does the woodcutter do with his wishes in "The Woodcutter"?

He uses them by wishing things that he should not wish for.

How does the woodcutter feel about his wishes at the end of the story?

He feels guilty and ashamed of the wishes he asked for

11 **Write an Extended Response** What lesson do you learn in both "The Stonecutter" and "The Woodcutter"? What do both the stonecutter and the woodcutter learn from making their wishes? Include details from the story that help teach that lesson.

_____

_____

_____

_____

_____

_____

_____

_____

_____

_____

_____

_____

_____

_____

Glossary

A

ax a tool used for chopping wood: *The woman used the **ax** to split logs into firewood.*

B

bale material that is pressed together and tied: *Large **bales** of paper were stacked against the wall.*

barely hardly; almost not: *He could **barely** walk on the icy sidewalk.*

beam a long piece of wood or metal: *Wooden **beams** held up the ceiling.*

bin a box used for storing things: *The cans for the food drive were sorted into large **bins**.*

blink to open and close your eyes quickly: *Everyone **blinked** because of the bright lights.*

C

chalkboard a dark surface for writing on with chalk: *The students wrote their answers on small **chalkboards**.*

chore a small job that has to be done: *One of the girl's **chores** was to take out the garbage.*

cycle a series of events that happen over and over again in the same order: *The life **cycle** of a frog goes from egg to tadpole to adult frog.*

D

dare to do something you are afraid of: *We didn't **dare** go into the dark cave.*

delicious good to taste: *The crisp apples were **delicious**.*

F

fleece the woolly coat of a sheep: *The **fleece** from sheep is often used to make clothing.*

flick to move something quickly: *The horse **flicked** its mane to shake out the water.*

forgotten not remembered: *I had **forgotten** to lock the door.*

form to start or take shape: *A plan was **forming** in her mind.*

frustration a feeling of anger caused by not being able to do something: *We could see the coach's **frustration** when her team didn't follow directions.*

Glossary

gain to get something: *The king hoped to gain even more wealth.*

guest someone who is invited to a place or event: *My parents are having three guests for dinner.*

harness a set of straps used to connect an animal to something: *The wagon driver put a harness on each horse.*

harvest 1. crops that are gathered from the fields: *A good harvest can provide people with food for months.* **2.** to bring in crops from the field: *The farmer harvested the wheat and corn.*

haul to pull or carry: *The horses hauled the heavy cart behind them.*

heartbeat the action of a heart as it pumps blood: *The patient's heartbeat slowed after she rested.*

hitchhiker someone who travels by getting a ride with someone else: *The hitchhiker needed a ride because his car had broken down.*

hollow an empty space in something: *A squirrel peeked from the hollow of the tree.*

invention a new object or way of doing things: *Some inventions, such as cars and light bulbs, have made our lives easier.*

jingling making a light, ringing sound: *The tags on the dog's collar started jingling when the dog ran.*

landfill an area where trash is buried: *The city's landfills are just about full.*

magnificent very great or amazing: *The magnificent palace sat on top of a tall hill.*

medicine something used to treat an illness or get rid of pain: *The doctor gave the little girl medicine for her cough.*

merchant someone who buys and sells things: *The merchant sold spices and silk.*

million a very large amount; the number 1,000,000: *Dinosaurs lived millions of years before people.*

mirror glass that reflects, or sends back, an image: *The kitten saw itself in the bathroom mirror.*

motor a machine that makes something move or work: *The car's motor was making a strange sound.*

muscle tissue that helps body parts to move: *We could see the horse's strong leg muscles when it ran.*

operation **1.** a set of planned actions: *Hundreds of people took part in a special operation to save the trapped whales.* **2.** A process where a doctor cuts into someone's body in order to fix a damaged part: *The patient needed an operation on his heart.*

orchard a place where fruit trees are grown: *We passed a large apple orchard.*

papaya a yellowish-green fruit: *The papaya is shaped like a pear.*

parachuter someone who jumps from a high place and floats to earth using special equipment: *The parachuter landed safely after jumping from a plane.*

platform a flat surface on which people or things can stand: *The band played on a raised platform.*

pod the part of a plant that holds seeds: *The pods of some plants burst open in the fall.*

prehistoric anything that lived or took place before people could write: *We can learn about prehistoric animals by studying their bones.*

propeller a set of flat spinning blades that make a plane or ship move forward: *The boat's propellers got caught in the weeds.*

quill a long hollow tube on the back of a porcupine: *The porcupine's sharp quills keep it safe from other animals.*

Glossary

recycle to make something new from something that has been used before: *Those chairs are made from **recycled** plastic bottles.*

reflection the image seen in a mirror or shiny surface: *I could see my **reflection** in the window.*

refraction the bending of light: *A rainbow is caused by **refraction** of sunlight on raindrops.*

ripe fully grown and ready for eating: *The bowl was filled with **ripe** green grapes.*

sap a watery juice inside a plant: *Sweet **sap** flows through the trunks and branches of trees.*

scarlet a bright red color: *The bird's **scarlet** feathers made it easy to see.*

scraps bits of leftover food: *We collected the **scraps** from our meal and fed them to the animals.*

seesaw a long flat board, balanced in the middle, that children play on: *My sister and I played on the **seesaw** until we were both tired.*

settle to place in a comfortable position: *The deer **settled** itself onto a pile of leaves.*

shallow not deep: *I stayed in the **shallow** end of the pool.*

sight a famous or interesting place: *The tour bus went to the most popular **sights** in the city.*

skim to move quickly near the surface of something: *The geese **skimmed** over the lake before finally landing.*

sprout to grow: *Seeds begin to **sprout** when the weather warms up.*

stretch to make something longer: *She **stretched** her arms above her head.*

survive to remain alive: *Animals need food and a place to live to **survive** a bad winter.*

sweeping wide; including many things: *I had a **sweeping** view of the park from the top of the hill.*

swoop to fly down suddenly: *The owl **swooped** down from the tree branch.*

syrup a sweet, sticky liquid added to food: *I like lots of **syrup** on my pancakes.*

temperature a measurement of how much heat is in a person's body: *His temperature showed he had a fever.*

tolerate to deal with or allow to continue: *My dad could no longer tolerate the loud music from next door.*

town square a place near the center of a town where people meet: *The fair was held in the town square.*

trash things that have been thrown away: *The garbage cans were filled with trash.*

treaty an agreement between people or groups: *After the war, the two countries signed a peace treaty.*

tremble to shake with fear: *The thunder made our dog tremble.*

view everything that can be seen from a certain spot: *The view from the top of the tower was amazing.*

vine a plant with a very long stem: *The vine wrapped around the tree trunk.*

voyage a long trip, usually over water: *Long ago, a sea voyage could last over a year.*

warehouse a large building used to store things: *The company kept its products in a nearby warehouse.*

waste things that are not wanted: *The city collects yard waste like leaves and grass clippings to be recycled.*

wedge to push into a tight space: *We tried to wedge all the boxes into the tiny closet.*

wingspan the distance from the tip of one wing to the tip of the other: *The wingspan of a bald eagle can be over seven feet.*

Language Handbook

Table of Contents

Nouns

LAFS.2.L.1.1: Demonstrate command of the conventions of standard English grammar and usage when writing or speaking.

Introduction

A **noun** is a word that names a person, place, or thing.

- A **common noun** names any person, place, or thing.
- A **proper noun** names a certain person, place, or thing. It begins with a capital letter.

	Common Nouns	**Proper Nouns**
Person	boy, aunt	Daniel, Aunt Maria
Place	street, store	King Street, Super Toy Shop
Thing	dog, game	Sparky, Crazy Cards

Guided Practice

Underline the noun or nouns in each sentence. Then write each noun in the chart to tell what it names.

HINT A proper noun can be more than one word. Each important word in a proper noun begins with a capital letter.

1. Uncle Marco needs a new hat.

2. We take the bus to the Top Shop.

3. A woman sells us a green Cappy Cap.

4. We leave the store and walk to the park.

Person	Place	Thing
Uncle marco woman	top shop Store park	hat bus Cappy cap

Independent Practice

Choose the correct word or words to answer each question.

1 Which words in this sentence are **nouns**?

My friends went to the mall.

A   friends, went

B   My, friends

C   friends, mall

D   went, mall

2 Which noun in this sentence names a **person**?

Lilly got a new shirt for school.

A   Lilly

B   new

C   shirt

D   school

3 Which noun in this sentence names a **place**?

Raj got a big pretzel at the Snacky Shack.

A   Raj

B   big

C   pretzel

D   Snacky Shack

4 Which noun in this sentence names a **thing**?

Cleo got a gift for her friend Pablo.

A   Cleo

B   gift

C   friend

D   Pablo

Plural Nouns

LAFS.2.L.1.1c: Form and use frequently occurring irregular plural nouns (e.g., *feet, children, teeth, mice, fish*).

Introduction

A **singular noun** is a noun that names one person, place, or thing. A **plural noun** names more than one person, place, or thing.

- You can form the plural of most nouns by adding **-s** or **-es**.

Singular	bird	glass	bush	fox
Plural	birds	glasses	bushes	foxes

- Some plurals change in special ways or do not change at all. You just have to remember them.

	Change in Special Ways					
Singular	child	foot	tooth	mouse	goose	man
Plural	children	feet	teeth	mice	geese	men

	Do Not Change			
Singular	deer	fish	moose	sheep
Plural	deer	fish	moose	sheep

Guided Practice

Write the plural of the noun to complete each sentence.

HINT If a noun ends in **tch**, add **-es** to make it plural.

Example:
ditch + es =
ditches

1. Two _Children_ walk in the woods.
   child

2. They hop over some _Patches_ of mud.
   patch

3. Do you see those _tracks_ in the dirt?
   track

4. This animal has four _feet_.
   foot

Independent Practice

Choose the correct plural of the noun to complete each sentence.

1 The pond is full of many _____ .

(A) fish

B fishs

C fishes

D feesh

2 Six _____ swim on the water.

A gooses

B geeses

(C) geese

D goose

3 Three _____ live near the pond.

A mices

B mouse

C mouses

(D) mice

Read the sentence. Circle the plural noun that is spelled incorrectly. Then write the word correctly.

4 Three (childs) saw five moose through the trees and bushes.

Children

Lesson 3
Collective Nouns

LAFS.2.L.1.1b: Use collective nouns (e.g., *group*).

Introduction A **noun** names a person, place, or thing. Some nouns name groups of people, animals, or other things that go together.

a **crowd** of people

a **herd** of buffalo

a **pack** of wolves

a **bunch** of bananas

a **pile** of leaves

a **school** of fish

a **swarm** of bees

a **flock** of birds

Guided Practice Circle the noun that names a group in each sentence.

HINT A noun that names a group often comes before the word *of*.

1 A herd of cows stood in the field.

2 The horse ate a bunch of carrots.

3 The dog chased a flock of geese.

4 The chickens pecked at a pile of seeds.

5 A swarm of flies buzzed around the pigs.

6 A crowd of children watched the sheep.

Independent Practice

Choose the correct word to answer each question.

1 Which word can name a group of dogs?

A   flock

B   swarm

C   pack

D   bunch

2 Which word can name a group of sticks?

A   herd

B   school

C   swarm

D   pile

3 Which noun correctly completes this sentence?

I see a _____ of fish swimming in the pond.

A   school

B   herd

C   pile

D   flock

Write the best word from the box to complete the sentence.

| flock |
| bunch |
| crowd |
| swarm |

4 The farmer picked a

_____bunch_____ of grapes.

Lesson 4
Pronouns

LAFS.2.L.1.1: Demonstrate command of the conventions of standard English grammar and usage when writing or speaking.

Introduction
A **pronoun** is a word that takes the place of a noun. Pronouns can be **singular** or **plural**.

- Some pronouns take the place of a noun that tells who or what does something.

  He   They   It
  ~~Sam~~ plays. ~~Sam's friends~~ sing. ~~The music~~ sounds great.

Singular (One)					Plural (More Than One)		
I	you	he	she	it	we	you	they

- Some pronouns take the place of a noun that follows an action word. They might come after a word such as *to*, *for*, or *from*.

  it   them
  Sam plays ~~guitar~~. Sam plays for ~~Mr. and Mrs. Chung~~.

Singular (One)					Plural (More Than One)		
me	you	him	her	it	us	you	them

Guided Practice
Circle the pronoun that can take the place of the underlined word or words.

HINT A plural pronoun can take the place of two or more words.

Example:
Boys and girls play music.
They play music.

1. The class learns from <u>Mr. Chung</u>.   (him)   he   them

2. <u>Katya</u> plays the piano.   (She)   It   Her

3. David plays <u>the tuba</u>.   them   (it)   us

4. <u>Timor and Liz</u> play horns.   Them   He   (They)

5. They play for <u>Maya and me</u>.   we   her   (us)

Independent Practice

Choose the pronoun that can take the place of the underlined word or words.

1 <u>Simon</u> blows the horn.

  A They

  B We

  C Him

  D He

2 Haley pounds on <u>the drum</u>.

  A it

  B them

  C him

  D me

3 <u>Maya and I</u> stomp our feet.

  A You

  B We

  C It

  D Us

4 Mr. Chung covers <u>his ears</u>!

  A they

  B it

  C them

  D her

Lesson 5
Reflexive Pronouns

LAFS.2.L.1.1d: Use reflexive pronouns (e.g., *myself, ourselves*).

Introduction

A **pronoun** is a word that takes the place of a noun. A **reflexive pronoun** refers back to a noun or pronoun at the beginning of a sentence. Reflexive pronouns end in *-self* or *-selves*. They can refer back to singular or plural nouns or pronouns.

Eva drew **herself**.   We painted pictures of **ourselves**.

Singular (One)	myself, yourself, himself, herself, itself
Plural (More Than One)	ourselves, yourselves, themselves

Guided Practice

Choose the reflexive pronoun that refers back to the underlined word in each sentence. Write the reflexive pronoun that correctly completes the sentence.

HINT Reflexive pronouns usually come after action words or after words such as *by, to, of,* and *on*.

| myself | yourself | himself | itself | themselves |

1   I drew a picture of _Myself_.

2   Some <u>children</u> spilled paint on _thamselve_.

3   <u>Leo</u> almost cut _himself_ with the scissors.

Independent Practice

Choose the correct pronoun to complete each sentence.

1. Nelly got _____ some clay.

   A myself

   B yourself

   (C) herself

   D itself

2. I covered _____ with a smock.

   A herself

   B ourselves

   C himself

   (D) myself

3. We made clay pots for _____.

   A himself

   B themselves

   (C) ourselves

   D itself

Write the correct pronoun from the box to complete the sentence.

| himself |
| themselves |
| yourselves |

4. The boys worked quietly by

   Themselves .

Lesson 6
Verbs

LAFS.2.L.1.1: Demonstrate command of the conventions of standard English grammar and usage when writing or speaking.

Introduction

A **verb** is a word that tells what someone or something does or is. A verb can tell what is happening now.

- An **action verb** tells what someone or something **does**.

I **throw** the ball.

The ball **drops** through the hoop.

- A **linking verb** tells what someone or something **is** or **is like**. The words *is, are,* and *am* are linking verbs.

Chrissy **is** our tallest player.

Are all basketball players tall?

I **am** on a basketball team.

Guided Practice

Circle the verb in each sentence.

HINT The linking verbs *is, are,* and *am* can be the first word of a question.

Example:
Is the game over?

1 This game is exciting.

2 Our players run down the court.

3 Chrissy catches the ball.

4 She jumps high.

5 The ball bounces on the rim.

6 Are we the winners?

Independent Practice

Choose the word that answers each question.

1 Which word in this sentence is a **verb**?

Jacob and Chrissy are the best players.

A   Jacob

B   are

C   best

D   players

2 Which word in this sentence is a **verb**?

Our team wins every basketball game.

A   team

B   wins

C   every

D   game

3 Which of these words is an **action verb**?

The crowd cheers when the game is over.

A   cheers

B   game

C   is

D   over

4 Which word in this sentence is a **linking verb**?

I am so happy!

A   happy

B   I

C   am

D   so

Samuel Dominguez

Lesson 7
Past Tense of Irregular Verbs

LAFS.2.L.1.1e: Form and use the past tense of frequently occurring irregular verbs (e.g., *sat, hid, told*).

Introduction A **verb** tells what someone or something does or is. A **past-tense verb** shows an action that happened in the past.

- The letters *-ed* at the end of a verb show an action that happened in the past.

  Today, I **walk** to the pool. Yesterday, I **walked** to the pool.

- Some verbs are **irregular**. They change in special ways to show an action that happened in the past. You just have to remember these.

  Today, I **go** to the pool. Yesterday, I **went** to the pool.

Now	sit	come	get	see	tell	run
In the Past	sat	came	got	saw	told	ran

Guided Practice Circle the correct past-tense verb to complete each sentence.

HINT Use the chart to find the correct spelling of each irregular past-tense verb.

1. Last week, I __saw__ Aldo at the pool. sees   (saw)

2. We __sat__ by the side of the pool. (sat)   sits

3. Then we __jumped__ into the water. jumps   (jumped)

4. Aldo __told__ me he was cold. (told)   telled

5. We __got__ out of the cold water. getted   (got)

Independent Practice

Choose the correct past-tense verb.

1 Yesterday, Shia _____ to the beach.

   A   go

   B   goes

   C   went

   D   goed

2 Tommy _____ to the beach with me last week.

   A   came

   B   come

   C   comed

   D   camed

3 The life guard _____ in a tall chair.

   A   sit

   B   sited

   C   sate

   D   sat

4 Mom _____ me to be careful in the water.

   A   told

   B   toll

   C   tell

   D   teld

Lesson 8
Adjectives and Adverbs

LAFS.2.L.1.1f: Use adjectives and adverbs, and choose between them depending on what is to be modified.

Introduction An **adjective** is a word that tells more about a noun. Adjectives usually tell "what kind" or "how many."

My jacket is **green**.   It has **two** pockets.

What Kind	red, loud, old, sweet, happy
How Many	one, ten, few, some, many

An **adverb** is a word that tells more about a verb.

- Adverbs often tell "how." These adverbs usually end in -ly.

I **quickly** zip my jacket.   I tie my shoes **tightly**.

- Adverbs can also tell "when" or "where."

I **soon** leave.   I run **outside**.

How	slowly, loudly, lightly, carefully
When	later, next, soon, yesterday
Where	there, nearby, somewhere

Guided Practice Write "adjective" or "adverb" to name each underlined word. Then circle the noun or verb that it tells about.

HINT Adjectives and adverbs do not always go beside the word they tell about.

1. Tia has lost her <u>purple</u> scarf. _Adjective_

2. She wore it to school <u>yesterday</u>. _adverb_

3. <u>Two</u> friends look for it. _adjective_

4. They look <u>everywhere</u>. _adverb_

Independent Practice

Choose the word that answers each question.

1 Which word in this sentence is an **adjective**?

The friends quickly find the purple scarf.

A purple

B scarf

C find

D quickly

2 Which word in this sentence is an **adverb**?

Tia thanks her good friends gladly.

A good

B thanks

C friends

D gladly

Write the correct word from the box to complete each sentence.

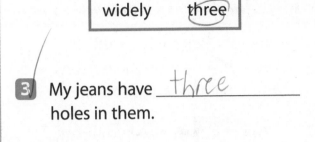

widely	three

3 My jeans have _three_ holes in them.

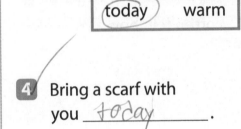

today	warm

4 Bring a scarf with you _today_.

Lesson 9
Complete Sentences

LAFS.2.L.1.1: Demonstrate command of the conventions of standard English grammar and usage when writing or speaking.

Introduction A **sentence** is a group of words that tells a complete thought.

- Every sentence has a **subject**. The subject names the person or thing that the sentence is about.

  > subject
  > **The children** play in the park.

- Every sentence has a **predicate**. The predicate tells what the subject does or is.

  > predicate
  > They **love the big playground**.

- A sentence begins with a **capital letter**. It ends with a **period**.

Guided Practice Read each sentence. Above the underlined words, write "S" for "Subject" or "P" for "Predicate."

> **HINT** The subject can name more than one person or thing.

1 <u>The kids</u> run on the playground.

2 Gracie <u>goes down the slide</u>.

3 Two children <u>swing from the bars</u>.

4 <u>Mom and Uncle Ray</u> sit on a bench.

5 A black dog <u>runs across the playground</u>.

Independent Practice

Choose the correct group of words to answer each question.

1 What is the **subject** of this sentence?

Two teams play kickball.

A   play kickball

B   teams play

C   Two teams

D   kickball

2 What is the **predicate** of this sentence?

Kevin and Maria chase the ball.

A   chase the ball

B   Kevin and Maria chase

C   Kevin and Maria

D   the ball

3 Which of these is a complete sentence?

A   The red ball.

B   Rolls into a puddle.

C   Right into a big puddle.

D   The ball rolls into a puddle.

4 Which of these is a complete sentence?

A   The cute little dog.

B   The dog stands by the ball.

C   The little dog and the red ball.

D   Stands by the red ball.

Language Handbook Lesson 9 Complete Sentences   **417**

Lesson 10
Simple and Compound Sentences

LAFS.2.L.1.1g: Produce, expand, and rearrange complete simple and compound sentences (e.g., *The boy watched the movie; The little boy watched the movie; The action movie was watched by the little boy*).

🐾 **Introduction** A **sentence** is a group of words that tells a complete thought.

• A **simple sentence** has <u>one subject</u> and <u>one predicate</u>.

> subject predicate
> **Many people** love pets.

• A **compound sentence** is <u>two simple sentences</u> joined together by a word such as *or, and,* or *but.*

> simple sentence   simple sentence
> Luis likes dogs, **but** Helen likes cats.

🐾 **Guided Practice** Write a joining word to complete each compound sentence.

and	but	or

HINT Place a comma before the joining word.

1. Helen feeds her cat Leo, _and_ she plays with him.

2. Leo likes chicken, _but_ he likes fish better.

3. Leo naps on a chair, _or_ he sleeps in his bed.

4. Helen's sister wants a snake, _but_ Dad does not like snakes.

5. He likes turtles, _and_ he loves frogs.

6. Leo might like a frog, _or_ he might scare it.

Independent Practice

Choose the correct way to join the two simple sentences.

1 Anna got a frog. She put it in a tank.

A Anna got a frog and, she put it in a tank.

B Anna got a frog, and, she put it in a tank.

C Anna got a frog, she put it in a tank.

D Anna got a frog, and she put it in a tank.

2 The frog eats many things. It does not like vegetables.

A The frog eats many things, but, it does not like vegetables.

B The frog eats many things, but it does not like vegetables.

C The frog eats many things, it does not like vegetables.

D The frog eats many things but, it does not like vegetables.

3 Leo will watch the frog quietly. He will meow at it.

A Leo will watch the frog quietly or, he will meow at it.

B Leo will watch the frog, quietly or he will meow at it.

C Leo will watch the frog quietly, or he will meow at it.

D Leo will watch the frog quietly, he will meow at it.

Underline the two simple sentences in the compound sentence. Circle the joining word.

4 Helen picks up Leo, and she takes him away.

Capitalization in Holidays, Product Names, and Geographic Names

LAFS.2.L.1.2a: Capitalize holidays, product names, and geographic names.

Introduction

The names of **holidays, products,** and **places** like towns, states, and countries are proper nouns. Use capital letters correctly when you write them.

- Begin each word of a holiday, product, or place with a capital letter.
- Do not begin words such as *for* and *of* with a capital letter.

Holidays	**T**hanksgiving, **P**residents' **D**ay, **F**ourth of **J**uly
Products	**S**peedy **S**neakers, **K**ites for **K**ids, **T**ummy **Y**ums
Places	**H**illtown, **N**orth **C**arolina, **U**nited **S**tates of **A**merica

Guided Practice

Read each sentence. Write the name of each underlined holiday, product, or place correctly.

HINT The word *day* is part of the name of many holidays. Remember to begin it with a capital letter.

1 The <u>fourth of july</u> is a fun holiday.

Fourth of July

2 People in the <u>united states of america</u> celebrate every year.

United States of America

3 Some cities, such as <u>boston</u>, have fireworks.

Boston

4 My family eats treats called <u>freezy pops</u>.

Freezy Pops

5 This holiday is also called <u>independence day</u>.

Independence Day

Independent Practice

Choose the correct way to write the underlined words in each sentence.

1 Two other American holidays are Thanksgiving and flag day.

  A flag day

  B flag Day

  C Flag day

  D Flag Day

2 The city of new orleans has parades on some holidays.

  A New orleans

  B new Orleans

  C New Orleans

  D new orleans

3 Kids blow loud horns called happy honkers.

  A Happy honkers

  B Happy Honkers

  C happy Honkers

  D happy honkers

Read the sentence. Circle the three words that should begin with a capital letter.

4 I like to stay up late on new year's eve.

Lesson 12
Punctuating Greetings and Closings of Letters

LAFS.2.L.1.2b: Use commas in greetings and closings of letters.

Introduction When you write a letter to someone, you begin with a **greeting**. You end with a **closing**.

greeting →	Dear Nana, Thank you for the scooter. It is my favorite gift!

closing →	Yours truly, Trina

- Use a **comma** (,) after the greeting and closing of a letter.

Guided Practice Add commas where they belong in the first two letters. Then write a closing for the third letter.

HINT When you write a greeting or closing, you begin the first word with a capital letter.

1 Dear Bin,

I got a red bike for my birthday! Can you come visit?

Your friend,

Harold

2 Dear Harold,

I hope to visit soon. I want to ride your new bike!

Best wishes,

Bin

3 Dear Tracy,

I got a letter from Bin. He may visit soon!

Yours truly,

Harold

©Curriculum Associates, LLC   Copying is not permitted.

Independent Practice

Read each question. Then choose the correct answer.

1 How should this **greeting** be written?

Dear Mr. Gomez

A   Dear Mr. Gomez?

B   Dear, Mr. Gomez,

C   Dear, Mr. Gomez

D   Dear Mr. Gomez,

2 How should this **closing** be written?

Very truly yours

A   Very truly yours,

B   Very truly yours!

C   Very truly yours.

D   Very truly yours

Read the letter. Then rewrite the greeting and closing correctly.

Dear, Papa

Thank you for the book. I can't wait to find out how it ends.

Lots of love.
Rachel

3 Dear Papa,

4 Lots of love,

Lesson 13
Contractions

LAFS.2.L.1.2c: Use an apostrophe to form contractions . . .

Introduction A **contraction** is a short way of putting two words together.

- When you write a contraction, you leave one or more letters out.

  I + am = **I'm**   I'm strong and healthy.

- An **apostrophe** (') takes the place of the missing letters.

she + **is** = she's	do + n**o**t = don't
we + **wi**ll = we'll	does + n**o**t = doesn't
is + n**o**t = isn't	did + n**o**t = didn't
can**no**t = can't	are + n**o**t = aren't

Guided Practice Read each sentence. Write a contraction for the underlined word or words.

HINT To form most contractions, drop only the vowel of the second word. But for *cannot* and contractions with *will,* drop the consonant before the vowel, too.

can**no**t = can't

we **wi**ll = we'll

1 <u>I am</u> making muffins with my sister. ___I'm___

2 <u>She is</u> a good baker. ___She's___

3 <u>We will</u> use butter and eggs. ___we'll___

4 We <u>cannot</u> forget the flour! ___can't___

5 I <u>do not</u> want nuts in the muffins. ___don't___

6 My brother <u>does not</u> like nuts either. ___doesn't___

Independent Practice

Read each question. Choose the correct answer.

1 Which contraction for "did not" is written correctly?

  A   didnt'

  B   di'dnt

  C   didn't

  D   did'not

2 Which contraction for "we will" is written correctly?

  A   we'll

  B   we'ill

  C   well'

  D   we'l

3 Which contraction for "she is" is written correctly?

  A   she'is

  B   she's

  C   shes'

  D   shes

Read the sentence. Circle the contraction that is not written correctly.

4 Dad can't find the box of raisins. It is'nt on the shelf.

Isn't

Possessive Nouns

LAFS.2.L.1.2c: Use an apostrophe to form . . .
frequently occurring possessives.

Introduction A **possessive noun** names a person or thing that something belongs to.

> a tail belonging to a whale = a whale's tail

A possessive noun has an **apostrophe (')**.

- If a noun is <u>singular</u>, add an apostrophe and **-s** to the end of the word.

> **whale + 's** = A whale's tail is very strong.

- If a noun is <u>plural</u> and already ends with **-s**, just add the apostrophe after the **-s**.

> **whales + '** = Look at those whales' tails!

Guided Practice Add an apostrophe and -s or just an apostrophe to make the correct possessive noun in each sentence.

HINT A plural noun names more than one person, place, or thing, and usually ends with -s.

1 A whale's___ baby is called a calf.

2 The two babies'___ faces are very cute.

3 The three scientists'___ job is to study whales.

4 Special fat keeps these animals'___ bodies warm.

5 A whale does not have teeth like a shark's___ teeth.

Independent Practice

Choose the correct way to write each underlined noun.

1 <u>Lindas</u> teacher told the class about whales.

A Lindas'

B Linda's

C Lindas's

D Linda's'

2 The <u>teachers</u> photos of whales were amazing.

A teachers's

B teache'rs

C teachers

D teacher's

3 Many <u>students</u> reports had drawings of whales.

A students'

B students's

C student's

D students

Write the correct word from the box to complete the sentence.

Jason's'

Jason's

Jasons's

Jasons

4 _Jason's_ mother studies sharks.

Lesson 15
Spelling Patterns

LAFS.2.L.1.2d: Generalize learned spelling patterns when writing words (e.g., cage → badge; boy → boil).

Introduction Some vowel sounds can be spelled more than one way.

- The vowel sound you hear in *boy* can be spelled **oy** or **oi**. Use **oy** if the sound is at the end of the word. Use **oi** if it is in the middle.

  | boy | joy | toy | boil | noise | coin |

- The vowel sound you hear in *day* can be spelled **ay** or **ai**. Use **ay** if the sound is at the end of the word. Use **ai** if it is in the middle.

  | day | play | spray | train | wait | paint |

Guided Practice Circle the correct letter pair that completes each word. Then write it on the line.

HINT Use **ai** or **oi** if the vowel sound is at the beginning of the word.

Examples:

aid   **oi**nk

1 The b_____ rides a red scooter.   **oy**   **oi**

2 The wheels make a strange n_____se.   **oy**   **oi**

3 He uses _____l to stop the squeak.   **oy**   **oi**

4 He may p_____nt his scooter blue.   **ay**   **ai**

5 Maybe he can spr_____ it on.   **ay**   **ai**

Independent Practice

Choose the correct way to spell the missing word in each sentence.

1 The sky is stormy and very _____ .

A gray

B grai

C graiy

D gra

2 The bad weather may _____ the hike.

A spoyl

B spoil

C spail

D spoyil

Write the correct spelling of the underlined word in each sentence.

3 The <u>rayn</u> comes down hard.

_____

4 I do not <u>enjoi</u> this weather.

_____

Using a Dictionary to Check Spelling

LAFS.2.L.1.2e: Consult reference materials, including beginning dictionaries, as needed to check and correct spellings.

Introduction

A **dictionary** lists words and their meanings. The words are shown in **alphabetical order**, or from **A** to **Z**. The **guide words** at the top of each page tell the first and last word on the page.

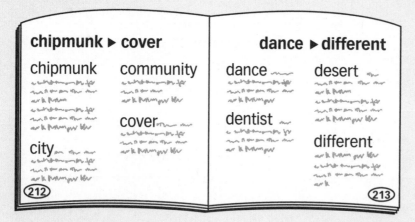

You can use a dictionary to check a word's spelling. First, find a page that shows words with the same **first** **letter** as your word. Use the guide words to help you. Next, look at the **second** **letter** of each word to see if yours comes before or after it.

Guided Practice

Check the spelling of each underlined word. Write the correct spelling on the line.

HINT Look at the guide words on each page. If your word comes between them in the alphabet, it is on that page.

1 A <u>comunity</u> is where you live. _Community_

2 Many people live and work in a <u>citty</u>. _City_

3 Workers do <u>differrint</u> jobs. _different_

4 A <u>dentest</u> takes care of teeth. _dentist_

Independent Practice

Use a dictionary to check the spelling of each underlined word. Then choose the correct spelling.

1 Some workers wear special <u>clohse</u> and hats.

A   clohs

B   clothes

C   cloths

D   clohz

2 The police keep people out of <u>danjer</u>.

A   danger

B   dainger

C   danjer

D   dangor

3 Firefighters must often <u>crall</u> through smoke.

A   crawll

B   crawle

C   crall

D   crawl

4 A <u>doctor</u> treats people who are sick or hurt.

A   doctur

B   docktor

C   docter

D   doctor

Language Handbook Lesson 16 Using a Dictionary to Check Spelling   **431**

Comparing Formal and Informal Uses of English

LAFS.2.L.2.3a: Compare formal and informal uses of English.

Introduction The words we use when we speak or write depend on whom we are speaking or writing to.

- We use "everyday" English with our friends and family. For example, we use short words and phrases called **slang** and **contractions**.

> Hi! What's up?
>
> I'm going to a movie. Can't wait!

- We use **formal** English with people we do not know well, or when we are in school. We use complete sentences and avoid slang and contractions.

> Hello, Mr. Chang. How are you?
>
> I am looking forward to the movie about pandas.

Everyday English	Formal English
yeah	yes
can't	cannot
Thanks a lot!	Thank you very much!
Sorry about that.	I apologize for my mistake.
All done!	I am finished.

Guided Practice Read each example of everyday English. Next to it, write the letter of the formal way to say it.

HINT *Don't* is a contraction of "Do not." *That's* is a contraction of "That is."

1 I don't get it. __C__

2 Best book ever! __d__

3 How's it going? __b__

4 Yup, that's right. __A__

a Yes, that is correct.

b How are you today?

c I do not understand.

d I liked this book very much.

Independent Practice

Choose the answer to each question.

1. What is the best way to greet an important person at your school?

A Hey.

B What's up, dude?

C Hi there!

D Hello.

2. Read this sentence from a book report. What is the best way to rewrite it?

> I can't believe the ending was so weird.

A I didn't like the ending. Not a bit.

B I found the ending difficult to believe.

C Boo, what a boring ending!

D I totally didn't get the ending.

3. Which word or words make the underlined word in this sentence more formal?

> This book is about why penguins <u>don't</u> fly.

A wanna

B are not gonna

C do not

D can't even

Rewrite the underlined words to be more formal.

4. Dear Captain Rodriguez,

I enjoyed your talk. <u>Thanks a bunch</u> for coming to our class.

Thanks a lot

Using Context Clues

LAFS.2.L.3.4a: Use sentence-level context as a clue to the meaning of a word or phrase.

Introduction When you see a word you don't know, look at the other words in the sentence. They can give you **clues** about what the word means.

- Sometimes other words in a sentence tell the **definition**, or meaning, of the word.

> definition
> The tops of trees in rain forests form a canopy, or **covering of leaves**.

- Sometimes other words in a sentence give an **example** that helps explain what the word means.

> example
> The forest canopy is like a **really big sun hat**.

Guided Practice Look at the underlined word in each sentence. Circle the other words that help you understand what the word means.

HINT Look for the words *or, like,* and *such as.* They often come before clues that help you figure out what a word means.

1 Many <u>creatures</u>, or animals, live in the rain forest.

2 Big <u>flocks</u>, or groups, of birds dive through the sky.

3 <u>Mammals</u>, like tigers and monkeys, climb on high branches.

4 Bright blue butterflies <u>flutter</u>, or fly, between tall trees.

5 Tiny <u>amphibians</u> such as frogs hide in the leaves.

6 <u>Enormous</u> snakes can be 30 feet long.

Independent Practice

Read the sentence below. Then answer the questions.

Big and small <u>nocturnal</u> animals only come out at night.

1 What do <u>nocturnal</u> animals do?

   A stay asleep all the time

   B come out when it gets dark

   C stay inside all the time

   D come out only during the day

2 Which words help you know what <u>nocturnal</u> means?

   A animals only

   B Big and small

   C only come out at night

   D animals come

Read the sentence below. Then answer the questions.

Wild cats hunt for <u>prey</u>, or food, after dark.

3 What does the word "prey" mean?

   A where wild cats live

   B when wild cats sleep

   C what wild cats look like

   D what wild cats eat

4 Which word helps you know what the word "prey" means?

   A cats

   B food

   C dark

   D wild

LAFS.2.L.3.4b: Determine the meaning of the new word formed when a known prefix is added to a known word (e.g., *happy/unhappy, tell/retell*).

🐾 Introduction You can use word parts to figure out what a word means.

A **prefix** is a word part added to the beginning of a word. It changes the meaning of the word.

Prefix	Meaning	Prefix + Word	New Word	Meaning
un-	"not"	un + fair	unfair	not fair
re-	"again"	re + tell	retell	tell again
pre-	"before"	pre + pay	prepay	pay before

🐾 Guided Practice

Look at the prefix in each underlined word. Then circle the correct meaning of the word.

HINT When you see a long word with a prefix, first look for a word you know in it. Then cover that word with your finger and look at the prefix. Think about what the prefix means and add the meaning to the word you know.

1 Dad and I are <u>unhappy</u> with our tree fort.

happy again   (not happy)

2 We will <u>rebuild</u> it.

(build again)   not build

3 The roof is broken and <u>unsafe</u>.

(not safe)   safe again

4 This time we will <u>preplan</u> how to build it.

not plan   (plan before)

5 We buy <u>precut</u> boards for the walls and roof.

(cut before)   not cut

Independent Practice

Look at the prefix in each underlined word. Then choose the correct meaning of the word.

1 We <u>redo</u> the walls of our fort.

A do again

B not do

C do before

D do wrong

2 We save the <u>unbroken</u> boards.

A broken again

B broken before

C very broken

D not broken

3 We <u>pretest</u> the old boards to be sure they are strong.

A test again and again

B do not test

C test before

D test later

4 We <u>repaint</u> the whole fort.

A not paint

B paint again

C paint quickly

D paint before

Root Words

LAFS.2.L.3.4c: Use a known root word as a clue to the meaning of an unknown word with the same root (e.g., *addition, additional*).

Introduction Some words can be broken into parts. The main part of the word is called a **root word**. The root word will help you figure out the meaning of the whole word.

For example, to help means to make it easier for someone to do something.

help	Ann will help us learn about weather.
helper	She is a great helper.
helpful	She is a very helpful person.
helping	She is helping us learn about clouds.

Guided Practice Circle the root word in each underlined word. Then draw a line from the sentence to the meaning of the word.

HINT If a word has an ending such as *-er* or *-y*, cover the ending with your finger, and read the smaller word. Think about what that word means.

1 Weather watchers study clouds.

people who look at something

2 Clouds give useful hints about weather.

getting dark

3 Puffy clouds mean the day will be nice.

helpful

4 Darkening clouds mean it might rain.

soft and light

Independent Practice

Look for the root word in each underlined word. Use this smaller word to help you answer the questions.

1 Read the sentence below.

Be <u>careful</u> when you see big, dark clouds.

What does the word "careful" mean in the sentence?

A quiet

B safe

C noisy

D silly

2 Read the sentence below.

<u>Dangerous</u> weather may be coming.

What does the word "Dangerous" mean in the sentence?

A good

B sunny

C cold

D harmful

3 Read the sentence below.

Bad weather can move <u>quickly</u>.

What does the word "quickly" mean in the sentence?

A fast

B soon

C slowly

D loudly

4 Read the sentence below.

Don't get caught in <u>stormy</u> weather!

What does the word "stormy" mean in the sentence?

A having lots of sunshine

B without clouds or rain

C with a lot of wind and rain

D with clear, blue skies

Compound Words

LAFS.2.L.3.4d: Use knowledge of the meaning of individual words to predict the meaning of compound words (e.g., *birdhouse, lighthouse, housefly; bookshelf, notebook, bookmark*).

Introduction A word that is made up of two smaller words is called a **compound** word.

Often you can figure out what a compound word means by thinking about the meanings of the two smaller words.

house   +   fly   = housefly

A housefly is a <u>fly</u> that gets into your <u>house</u>.

Guided Practice   Put the two words together to make a compound word. Write the new word on the line. Then circle the correct meaning.

HINT Sometimes the second word in the compound word is a big clue to the word's meaning. For example, a "dog**house**" is a house for a dog, not a dog that looks like a house.

1 black   +   bird   = _blackbird_
(a bird with black feathers)
a black feather shaped like a bird

2 sword   +   fish   = _swordfish_
a sword shaped like a fish
(a fish with a jaw like a sword)

3 rattle   +   snake   = _rattlesnake_
a rattle shaped like a snake
(a snake with a tail like a rattle)

Independent Practice

Read the compound word in each sentence. Then choose the correct meaning for the word.

1. A <u>catfish</u> uses its whiskers to find food in the sea.
   - A a fish that eats bugs
   - B a cat that looks like a bird
   - **C** a fish with whiskers like a cat
   - D a cat that likes boats

2. A <u>sheepdog</u> helps keep farm animals safe.
   - A a sheep used for its wool
   - **B** a dog that takes care of sheep
   - C a sheep that plays with birds
   - D a dog that looks like a goat

3. A <u>seahorse</u> has fins and swims in the ocean.
   - A a big ocean shaped like a horse
   - B a sea animal that looks like a snake
   - C a horse that lives in a barn
   - **D** a sea animal whose head looks like a horse

Choose one word from the box to complete the second sentence. Write the correct word on the line.

earthquake ~~earthworm~~ wormhole

4. The worm digs deep into the soil. This _earthworm_ crawls up out of the ground when it rains.

Lesson 22
Using a Dictionary

LAFS.2.L.3.4e: Use glossaries and beginning dictionaries, both print and digital, to determine or clarify the meaning of words and phrases.

Introduction A **dictionary** tells a word's **definition**, or what the word means. Some words have more than one meaning.

- How do you find the correct meaning of a word? Read each meaning to figure out which definition makes sense.
- Some dictionaries have sentences to help you understand the words.

what the word means   the word used in a sentence

block

1. a piece of wood or hard plastic used as a toy
My little sister lost the red block she was playing with.

2. an area of a city with streets on four sides
My best friend and I live in the same block.

Guided Practice Use the dictionary page above to find the correct meaning of each underlined word. Write the meaning on the line.

HINT Reread the sentence using the definition you chose. Does the sentence make sense?

1 Our class used <u>blocks</u> to make a model of our school.

_____

2 We walked around the <u>block</u> to look at the building.

_____

3 Our school takes up a whole city <u>block</u>!

_____

4 We used every <u>block</u> we had to build our model.

_____

Independent Practice

Use the dictionary below to answer each question. Write the meaning that makes sense in the sentence.

---

story

1. a group of words that tells about something real that happened
The story is about the first school in our city.

2. a floor or level in a building
The Empire State Building has 103 stories.

---

yard

1. an outside area near a house or building
Let's play in my yard after school.

2. an amount that tells how long something is
This short piece of rope is one yard long.

---

1 What does the word "story" mean in this sentence?

Our teacher read a <u>story</u> about how our school was built.

_____

_____

2 What does the word "story" mean in this sentence?

The school used to be only one <u>story</u> tall.

_____

_____

3 What does the word "yard" mean in this sentence?

Long ago, our school didn't have a <u>yard</u> around it.

_____

_____

4 What does the word "yard" mean in this sentence?

Now, our big playground is almost 50 <u>yards</u> wide.

_____

_____

Lesson 23
Using a Glossary

LAFS.2.L.3.4e: Use glossaries and beginning dictionaries, both print and digital, to determine or clarify the meaning of words and phrases.

Introduction Some books have a list of words called a **glossary**.

- A glossary is like a dictionary. It lists words in alphabetical order.
- It tells the meanings of important words in the book. Sometimes a glossary includes sentences that help you understand the word.
- You can often find the glossary near the end of a book.

> **gas** something like air that is so light it does not have a shape
> *Air is a gas we breathe.*
>
> **planet** a large ball-like object that moves around the sun
> *The Earth, where we live, is a planet.*
>
> **star** a small dot of light in the sky
> *I look for the brightest star in the sky.*

Guided Practice Use the glossary to find the meanings of the underlined words. Write the meanings on the lines.

HINT Use the first letter of the underlined word to help you find the word in the glossary.

1 Have you ever seen a <u>star</u> in the sky at night?

_____

2 It looks tiny from our <u>planet</u>, Earth.

_____

3 It really is a giant ball of hot <u>gas</u>.

_____

_____

Independent Practice

Use the glossary to find the meaning of each underlined word.

---

close near *My friend's house is close to mine.*

glowing shining *At night she could see her cat's glowing eyes.*

heat what makes things warm *I can feel the heat from the campfire.*

plant something that is alive but is not an animal or person *A tree is a plant.*

---

1 What does the word "glowing" mean in this sentence?

The sun is a large, <u>glowing</u> star.

A burning   **C** warm

B shining   **D** pretty

2 What does the word "close" mean in this sentence?

It looks big because it is <u>close</u> to Earth.

A above   **C** beside

B below   **D** near

3 What does the word "plants" mean in this sentence?

The sun helps <u>plants</u> grow.

A boys and girls

B living things

C dog and cats

D things that crawl

4 What does the word "heat" mean in this sentence?

It also gives off <u>heat</u> that keeps us warm.

A what makes things cold

B something that puts out a fire

C what makes things warm

D something that scares people

Real-Life Connections

LAFS.2.L.3.5a: Identify real-life connections between words and their use (e.g., describe foods that are *spicy* or *juicy*).

Introduction When you read, you can connect words to your own life to make their meaning clearer.

You read:	You might think:
Some things taste salty.	Salty popcorn makes me thirsty.
Some things sound loud.	My sister plays loud music.

Guided Practice Circle the correct word or words to complete each sentence.

> **HINT** Look at the answer choices. Ask yourself questions such as, "Have I ever eaten garlic? honey? ice? Which one tasted sweet?"

1 Something sweet might taste like _____.

garlic   ice   honey

2 Something quiet might sound like a _____.

fire alarm   whisper   thunderstorm

3 Something soft might feel like a _____.

kitten's fur   rock   bottle of water

4 Something round might look like a _____.

ball   flute   box

5 Something sweet might smell like a _____.

fish   flower   trash can

Independent Practice

Choose the correct answer to each question.

1 What is something you can <u>taste</u>?

   A a tall building

   B a juicy orange

   C a squeaky door

   D a sticky piece of tape

2 What is something you can <u>feel</u>?

   A a friend singing

   B a dinner cooking

   C a soft pillow

   D a TV show

3 What is something you can <u>smell</u>?

   A a honking horn

   B a cloud in the sky

   C a smooth sidewalk

   D a smoky fire

4 What is something you can <u>hear</u>?

   A a buzzing bee

   B a glass of milk

   C a piece of wood

   D a shining star

Lesson 25
Shades of Meaning

LAFS.2.L.3.5b: Distinguish shades of meaning among closely related verbs (e.g., *toss, throw, hurl*) and closely related adjectives (e.g., *thin, slender, skinny, scrawny*).

Introduction Some words have almost the same meanings, but some meanings are stronger than others. **Strong words** tell exactly or most clearly what is happening in a sentence.

- Think about which word shown in green is the strongest.

> We get up when we hear the fire alarm.
>
> We stand up when we hear the fire alarm.
>
> We jump up when we hear the fire alarm.

- The word *jump* is the strongest. It tells most clearly what the students do when they hear the alarm.

Not Strong	Stronger	Strongest
get	stand	jump

Guided Practice Read each pair of sentences. Look at the underlined words. Circle the word with the strongest meaning.

HINT Picture in your mind what happens during a fire drill. Choose the word that tells most clearly what is happening.

1. Ms. Diaz <u>says</u>, "It's a fire drill. Line up at the door."
   Ms. Diaz <u>shouts</u>, "It's a fire drill. Line up at the door."

2. We all feel a little <u>bad</u>.
   We all feel a little <u>scared</u>.

3. We <u>go</u> out to the playground.
   We <u>hurry</u> out to the playground.

4. Everyone on the <u>big</u> playground is quiet.
   Everyone on the <u>huge</u> playground is quiet.

Independent Practice

Circle the word in the box that best completes each sentence.

1 Read the sentence below.

The fire truck _____ up the street to the school.

Which word tells most clearly how fast the fire truck goes?

comes	races	moves	hurries

2 Read the sentence below.

_____ firefighters run into the school.

Which word tells exactly how many firefighters there are?

Some	Few	Several	Five

3 Read the sentence below.

Smiling, they _____ out the door of the school.

Which word tells most clearly how they leave the building?

come	march	move	walk

4 Read the sentence below.

This fire drill was _____!

Which word tells most clearly about how the fire drill went?

good	okay	excellent	fine

Lesson 26

Using Adjectives and Adverbs to Describe

LAFS.2.L.3.6: Use words and phrases acquired through conversations, reading and being read to, and responding to texts, including using adjectives and adverbs to describe (e.g., *When other kids are happy that makes me happy*).

🐾 **Introduction** When you write, choose **adjectives** and **adverbs** that make your ideas clear and interesting.

- Use the best adjective you know to tell about a noun. An **adjective** can tell how something looks, smells, tastes, sounds, or feels.

> Sue heard a squeaky noise.
>
> She smelled sweet muffins baking.
>
> Bright light came through the window.

- Use the best adverb you know to tell about a verb. An **adverb** can tell about how, where, or when something happens.

> Sue woke up late. ← when
>
> She dressed quickly. ← how
>
> She ran downstairs. ← where

🐾 **Guided Practice** Choose the adjective or adverb in parentheses ( ) that best completes each sentence. Write the word on the line.

HINT Try each answer choice in the sentence. Does the sentence make sense?

1 Sue hears a ___loud___ horn.
(loud   happy)

2 The bus came ___early___!
(tomorrow   early)

3 Sue grabs her ___heavy___ backpack.
(warm   heavy)

4 Dad says, "We have to run ___quickly___!"
(quickly   slowly)

👤 **Independent Practice**

Choose the correct word to complete each sentence.

1 The _____ school bus stops.

   A hungry

   B yellow

   C round

   D sleepy

2 Sue climbs _____ .

   A inside

   B after

   C down

   D outside

3 She finds an _____ seat.

   A excited

   B angry

   C unhappy

   D empty

4 She smiles and waves _____ to her dad.

   A meanly

   B noisily

   C happily

   D badly